Cherry Boone O'Neill

Starving for Attention

"A harrowing and near-tragic true story. A classic study that should be required reading."
—Gary Collins, host of *Hour Magazine,* ABC-TV

"As a parent who has experienced the problem of anorexia in our family, I cannot recommend this powerful book highly enough." —U.S. Senator Roger Jepsen

"A gripping true story. It gives more information about a growing national problem than a dozen medical textbooks. And it will help not only those suffering from anorexia—and their parents and friends—but countless young women caught up in the American obsession with weight and dieting."—Robert Mendelsohn, M.D.

Cherry Boone O'Neill is "a new Christian hero."
—William Griffen, *Publishers Weekly*

"A love story—sometimes chilling, sometimes heartwarming—in which faith, courage, and good psychiatry conquer the demon of self-hatred." —Andrew M. Greeley

"*Starving for Attention* will rivet the reader's attention. Ultimately, it is a moving affirmation of the value of family."
—Madeleine L'Engle

Process; self-esteem;
self-love. hope; secretiveness;
striving for perfection.

Starving
for
Attention

Cherry Boone O'Neill

A DELL BOOK

Published by
Dell Publishing Co., Inc.
1 Dag Hammarskjold Plaza
New York, New York 10017

Dell ® TM 681510, Dell Publishing Co., Inc.

ISBN: 0-440-17620-4

Reprinted by arrangement with Continuum Publishing,
a division of Crossroad Publishing Company

Printed in the United States of America

First Dell printing—October 1983

This book is written for

The people who endure the personal, hidden hell of anorexia nervosa;

Their family and friends who helplessly watch as their loved ones waste away;

And for hope, that they may emerge victorious from this nightmare.

With special thanks to

My sisters, Lindy, Debby, and Laury, for whom I care more than words can say;

My parents-in-law, Bill and Melba O'Neill, who loved me unconditionally as if I were their own;

My doctor, Ray Vath, who helped me learn to love myself and live appropriately;

And to God, for His endless grace and His gift of joy.

Most importantly, this book is dedicated to

My loving parents, Pat and Shirley Boone, who poured themselves out to give me life;

My giving husband, Dan, who loved me back to living;

And to my daughter, Brittany, who gives my life and love new meaning.

Contents

Preface

What would your reaction be if your child suddenly began to deteriorate before your eyes—apparently by her own doing? What would you do?

In the process of recovery from anorexia nervosa, I have had to ask myself this question in attempts to empathize with my parents. However, in the depths of the disease, I was unable to see myself realistically, so it stands to reason that only recently have I come to fully appreciate and understand the challenges my parents faced and the decisions they made.

This book, although written after my restoration to health, is written in part from perspectives I held during my ten-year illness in order to best shed light on this terrifying disorder—a sophisticated form of suicide that afflicts up to one million young women right now. The incidents and dialogue I have chosen to include reflect almost exclusively those environmental factors and personal experiences that contributed directly to my development of, and recovery from, anorexia. My narrative takes the evolving point of view of a person who becomes imprisoned by, and then ultimately freed from, invalid fears and misperceptions.

Consequently, you will not read about such positive times

as when my parents wholeheartedly involved themselves in creating our almost always award-winning Halloween costumes to wear in school competitions, when they spent hours assisting us on school projects, or their loving counsel in response to adolescent concerns. You will not be told of the times that my father would schedule his travels around a father-daughter dance, or how my mother would anticipate and meet our needs—often before they were even expressed. You won't read about the hugs, the kisses, and the tender "I love yous." But as you read about the problems, do bear in mind that the pleasant times greatly outweigh them and are more memorable and special to me by far.

As you begin this story, then, do not attempt to find fault in any individual, and remember that, by necessity, I have been selective in my autobiographical account. It is focused on one young woman's desperate struggle with a tenacious and potentially fatal disorder. Anorexia is a complex disease, and the only thing that any of us were ever guilty of was doing the best we could with what we knew.

I have, after all, had a wonderful life, with thanks to the many special people who have made it so—family, husband, doctors, friends. And I love them now all the more dearly for their humanness—for making occasional mistakes, but always trying to be helpful. Their selfless generosity and commitment even now fill my heart with gratitude and my eyes with tears.

CHERRY BOONE O'NEILL
Bothell, Washington

Prologue

"Merry Christmas, everybody!" I greeted relatives and friends as I descended into the sunken family room that was festive, bright, and brimming over with holiday wrapping, gifts on display and a multitude of cousins comparing Christmas outfits fresh out of their packages. I had just put on my new knit pantsuit to show off my slim seventeen-year-old figure to the assembled clan.

One nice thing about having lost all that weight: now I could fit into anything! After wearing tight clothes for a while, loose garments were a welcome relief. And these knit slacks not only felt nice, they showed off my hard-earned slender legs like merit badges. I'd managed to make it through the Thanksgiving feast and my pre-Christmas baking of cookies, breads, and cheesecakes to give as gifts without a single slip from my strict diet. And now there was the challenge of Christmas.

Fasting on Thanksgiving Day had really saved me. I hadn't had to make any decisions about what I could and couldn't eat, and when I was asked why I had not loaded up my plate like everyone else I just answered with spiritual overtones, "I'm fasting today," and that was that!

"Cherry, gather up all the kids and bring them into the

dining room,'' my mother called from the kitchen. ''Daddy wants to have Communion together before we say the blessing, okay?''

''Okay,'' I answered. As I went from room to room relaying my message to little people playing under the piano and inside closets, my mind was computing feverishly: crackers are about twelve calories and I'll probably eat about one twelfth, so that's one calorie, and grape juice—darn it! How much does that goblet hold and how many calories does a six-ounce glass of grape juice have? I forget. Too many. I'll just pretend to drink the grape juice. Hey, maybe I can pretend to eat the cracker, too! Then I can just smash it between my fingers and sprinkle the crumbs on the floor. No calories!

''Cherry, can you help bring in the salad and rolls?''

''Coming, Mama.'' I went into the kitchen and picked up the huge salad bowl and warm breadbasket. The scent of hot, fresh bread and roast turkey filled the room and made my head swim. Boy, does that smell good! *Too* good. But I couldn't fast again—two holidays in a row would look suspicious. I'd have to come up with something else.

While everyone was settled in their various locations, kids in the kitchen, ladies in the living room, men in the den with eyes riveted on images of flying pigskins, I surreptitiously made my way to one of the three refrigerators and found half a head of lettuce in a plastic bag. Perfect, I thought. I'll tell everyone I'm not hungry right now but reassure them of my plans to partake in the rich repast later, fully intending, of course, to skip it altogether. I plopped down in front of the television, feigning interest in the helmeted figures scrimmaging on the screen. Like a rabbit, I began nibbling on my Christmas dinner, leaf by leaf.

''Where's the rest of your meal, Cherry?'' Daddy asked.

My shoulders tensed as I felt his eyes burn into me like two laser beams.

I attempted to appear unaffected by his scrutiny and answered matter-of-factly, "Oh, I had some of that Christmas caramel corn earlier and it spoiled my appetite so I'm going to wait and get mine later." My eyes had never left the football game—about which I could not have cared less.

That night, I prepared for bed with a great sense of accomplishment. In the whirlwind of family activity no one noticed that I hadn't supplemented my meager excuse for a meal. Later, when my dad asked me if I had gotten my dinner, I deceptively assured him that I had eaten more than enough. Now that everyone is gone, I thought, I suppose I could go sneak a few bites without having to eat a whole meal. After all, it would be a shame not to at least taste all of those once-a-year goodies—turkey, stuffing, egg nog, and pecan pie.

As I opened the refrigerator door, my stomach growled with anticipation. That turkey skin looked crispy and full of buttery flavor. I pulled off a piece and placed it in my mouth, my salivary glands working double time as I slowly savored the first bite. As I looked back at the turkey, the missing skin resembling a gaping wound, I thought I'd better make it look less obviously ravaged. I pulled off the whole sheet of skin that lay across the breast to make it even. After all, I'd earned that much—I hadn't had anything but lettuce and coffee all day.

"Cherry, why don't you get a knife and cut yourself a slice and put it on a plate? Besides, I thought you told Daddy you'd already eaten." I jumped with surprise and embarrassment as I scrambled to stuff the handful of turkey skin in my mouth.

"Oh, I did!" I sputtered. "I'm just having a nibble, I don't want a whole slice." ·

"That looks like a lot more than a nibble to me!" My mother walked up to the refrigerator. She pulled back the foil I'd stretched back over the turkey and saw the "calling card" I left on her once beautiful bird.

"Cherry, how many times have I asked you not to eat off all of the skin? Other people like it too and no one likes to eat a turkey that's had somebody's fingers all over it! Now, I don't mind you eating—in fact, I'd love to see you eat more—but please get a plate and a fork and eat it like a human being."

"I told you, I don't want a whole plate!" I answered back. Blushing, I rinsed my hands and stormed out of the room.

Later that night, after my mother had gone to bed, I quietly snuck back to the kitchen determined to taste everything I'd missed. I grabbed a roll, dipped it into the gravy boat, and crammed it into my mouth. Then I ate some stuffing. Then a bite of a vegetable casserole. Next some pecans off the pie. Suddenly, I realized I'd gone too far. In two minutes I had destroyed an all-day effort to avoid eating. Well, no need to get depressed. I might as well eat my fill of everything now. I'll just have to get rid of it later. I knew how. I'd done it dozens of times before.

Mindlessly, I began shoveling handfuls of food into my mouth. I devoured huge amounts of leftovers from Christmas dinner, breakfast, and even from days before. Some of my cookies (crumbs first and then broken pieces before whole cookies), slivers of cherry-cream pie, a piece of pecan pie, tablespoons of ice cream, chocolate chip and jamoca-almond-fudge, more rolls with quarter-inch layers of butter, globs of peanut butter followed by spoonfuls of jam, and egg nog straight from the pitcher.

My distended stomach ached—I must have looked six months pregnant. My food frenzy began to slow down when I could no longer walk without bending over. Did I get everything I wanted? I guess so—besides I can't eat any more.

But wait! Some chocolates! I'll chew on those on the way upstairs with a glass of punch.

Once in my bathroom, I completed the now familiar ritual I'd begun this time with that first bite of turkey. I forced my finger down my throat. After several gut-wrenching heaves I regurgitated as much as I could until nothing but small amounts of bile, tinged pink with blood, emerged. I wiped off the toilet and began rinsing my beet-red face when I was startled by a hard knock on the door.

"Cherry, what's going on?" My father's voice was stern.

My heart pounded. "I'm just going to the bathroom. Why?" I quickly straightened my hair, sprayed air freshener, turned off the water.

"Open the door, Cherry. You know the rules about no locked doors in this house."

"You and Mommy lock your door sometimes," I answered back.

"Open this door, Cherry! Right now!"

"All right! All right! Just let me get my robe on," I stalled, trying to open the window for fresh air. Then I calmly unlocked and opened the door.

"It doesn't take you fifteen minutes to go to the bathroom, Cherry."

"I haven't been in here fifteen minutes," I lied.

"I was outside after taking a sauna and I looked up and

saw your bathroom light on. I waited, listened, and I know I heard you vomiting.'' His eyes glistened with anger.

"I did not! I swear! I was just going to the bathroom and washing my face!''

"Look here, Cherry,'' he said, gripping my arm and pulling me back into the bathroom. "Look at yourself! Your face is red, your eyes are bloodshot, the room stinks, and you're telling me you didn't throw up?''

"I didn't, Daddy! I promise I didn't! I was going to the bathroom. I've been constipated so my face gets red. Honest!'' My voice quavered with fear. Tears welled up in my eyes.

"Cherry, I don't understand this. I know you're lying, but it's late and I have to get up early. We should both be in bed—it's been a busy day. But don't think we aren't going to discuss this when I get back from Chicago! Now go to bed, and don't you get up again—for any reason!''

Suddenly he was gone and I stood alone in front of the mirror. I stared at my gaunt face, then burst into tears.

God, what's wrong with me? Why can't I control myself? If I just hadn't tasted that turkey! Then I wouldn't have gorged and had to throw up and lie to Daddy. But I had to eat *something!* I hadn't eaten all day! I usually have a bit of dinner, at least.

I looked at my swollen eyes as tears streaked down my hollow cheeks. I leaned against the door and slid down slowly as my whining turned to heaving, uncontrollable sobs.

You idiot! You liar! I thought, accusing myself. How can you expect God to help you when you can't even tell the truth! You can't even take Communion without worrying about calories!

I was sick of fighting with everyone. But I didn't know

what to do. I slumped to the floor in a heap. I began pounding my head with my fists. "God, take me, please! I can't handle this anymore! I don't want to live like this forever! Take me, please!" I sobbed convulsively. "God, I know I'm not worthy to even ask You for help when I'm the one doing this to myself. But I can't help it. Please, God, please help me find a way out of this horrible mess!"

Exhausted and weak, I drifted off to sleep on the vomit-stained carpet, half hoping I'd never wake up.

The idea of facing another day terrified me. The only thing that had kept me going this far was a faint, flickering, inner spark of hope—hope that somehow, some day, there would be the "way out" I so desperately needed. And that spark was fading fast.

I had no idea that I was slowly committing suicide.

CHAPTER ONE

Once Upon a Star

"I baptize you in the name of the Father, the Son, and the Holy Spirit." The water flowed from the clear vessel onto the smooth, well-shaped head bobbing about in response to the cool surprise. Father Ross Fewing, our parish priest, stretched his arms skyward, holding a lively, lovely three-month-old girl. Bringing her down slowly, he held her before the congregation. "Lord, we thank you for this gift from heaven You have given to us. I now introduce you to our new sister in the Lord, Brittany Anne Boone O'Neill." The people burst into applause, showing their enthusiasm for this newly received member of the family.

Family—that never-ending chain of life, each link unique, all of it miraculous. But this child was more than a miracle. She was once thought to be an impossibility.

As I returned to my seat with my husband, Dan, and our newly christened daughter, my moist eyes scanned the autumn-colored banners and stained glass. My thoughts raced back twenty-seven years and beyond to mental images of my own mother and father—a young married couple starting life together in a new city, expecting their first child and struggling to make ends meet.

* * *

July 7, 1954, 7:41 A.M. Flow Memorial Hospital, Denton, Texas. "Mr. Boone, your baby wanted to be born the hard way. Sideways! But we finally got her turned around and you've got yourself a healthy little girl."

The doctor's voice droned on but the young father heard nothing more. A girl? he thought. What about Michael Wayne? It was supposed to be a boy. That's all we talked about. I wonder if Shirley knows . . . Shirley! "Doctor, how's my wife?"

"Where have you been, Pat? I just told you she's doing great. Well, I guess a first-time Daddy's entitled to be excited. You can go see them now. They're both fine."

Being born a female was a real "attention getter." Mommy and Daddy had such high expectations for their "bouncing baby boy." It was an unquestioned assumption—part of a script.

And speaking of expectations, I had quite an illustrious heritage to live up to. My father, Charles Eugene "Pat" Boone, was the eldest son of Archie and Margaret Boone, his mom a registered nurse and his dad a foreman of the family construction company. Their lifestyle was modest but Archie Boone did take pride in the fact that his great-great-great grandfather was the frontiersman and trailblazer Daniel. My mother was born Shirley Lee Foley, oldest of three daughters, to country-singing star Red Foley and his wife, Eva, of the "Three Little Maids," a country-western sister trio.

At the ripe old age of nineteen, Pat Boone and Shirley Foley eloped and moved from their homes and families in Nashville, Tennessee, to Denton, Texas. Daddy enrolled in North Texas State College, studying to become an English teacher. Somehow they managed to pay the rent and care for their newborn baby on only $44.50 a week.

I'm told I was a cheerful baby with a quick smile that often seemed to swallow up my face in one big Cheshire Cat grin. And my parents were pleased at signs that I might be a precocious child—one of those kids who does everything before the doctor says it's time. Even before nursery school, I'd often lie down for a nap with a stack of encyclopedias to "read" myself to sleep. I guess my smile and my smarts convinced my parents that little girls were pretty nice to have around after all. Besides, they were only twenty years old; there would be plenty of time for little brothers.

Fourteen months later, another girl, Linda Lee, was born. But that wasn't the only change that had taken place. Lindy was born in New York City because the aspiring young English student had suddenly become a nationally known pop singer with three hit records and was now a member of the famous "Arthur Godfrey Show" family. (I was an honorary member myself but my job was to be cute—toddling around and calling for "Mr. Goppy.")

The road from Denton, Texas, to the Big Apple was virtually paved overnight. My dad had won the popular Ted Mack Amateur Hour contest. Even before he could compete in the finals, he was no longer an amateur because he had signed a contract with Dot Records and made his first recording in Chicago, entitled "Two Hearts, Two Kisses."

Success struck like a chain of explosives, uprooting our unassuming family and catapulting us across the country into a whole new world. Although he performed regularly on television, my dad was determined to finish school so he transferred to Columbia University, maintaining his speech and English majors. He seemed to me like Superman, and this was only the beginning.

In 1956, twenty-two-year-old Pat Boone had his own television series, "The Chevy Showroom," and a million-dollar contract with Twentieth Century-Fox. And Shirley Boone had daughter number three, Deborah Ann. Daddy's records kept striking gold and eventually we moved from a small house in Leonia, New Jersey, to a grand four-story Tudor in the lovely suburb of Teaneck. The front yard was a great green carpet in the summer, a white playground in winter—the perfect meeting place for all of the neighborhood kids, thirteen of whom lived next door. We had no gates, no fences—just a small assortment of huge, friendly looking old trees and rows of neatly sculpted shrubs. To a small child it was a king's castle, a fairy tale come true.

By 1958, Daddy graduated from Columbia *magna cum laude* and had five more gold records and a couple of movies under his belt. And yes, Laura Gene had come along to make Pat Boone a proud (if slightly disappointed) papa of four little girls. I've always felt my mother deserved a medal of valor for having four babies in three and a half years, not to mention adjusting to several major upheavals in lifestyle, including a marriage that had to be maintained by long distance for eighteen months out of their first three years as man and wife.

At the time, I was still a happy and precocious child, already "Mommy's little helper" by age four. I felt very responsible for my sisters and very proud of my position as the oldest: as firstborn, much was given me and so much was also expected. Mommy, of course, could only do so much at once so most of my privileges were actually necessities—from helping with the never-ending diapers to holding my sisters' hands when crossing streets. In my eagerness to win the approval of my parents and the admiration of my sisters, I performed my good-little-girl routine to the hilt. It made me feel valuable, loved, worth something. The praise and favorable comments it elicited were enough to motivate me to keep it up for life—almost. In fact, I had already become sensitive to the slightest hint that perhaps I wasn't measuring up to what I thought I was supposed to be in order to deserve love, acceptance, and praise.

My parents have told me of moments when my delicate ego would surface. One day my mother was scolding me for something, perhaps a bit more harshly than was warranted. My eyes teared up, my lower lip curled downward, and in a quivering voice I said, "You hurt my heart!" My desire to please extended even to God. At prayer time one night, I paused and asked, "Could You speak a little louder, God, I can't quite hear You!"

I remember my first piano recital. I was only four years old when I started my lessons and I was to play the piece I had practiced and memorized for an audience of fifty parents. I can still recall the feeling of pride as I walked out on that stage in my patent-leather shoes and petticoated pinafore, with white gloves and bright eyes. I sat down at the baby grand, my feet dangling high above the pedals. I began to perform. As my confidence increased, I beamed out at the appreciative crowd. Their approval brought me great joy which bubbled over into a gleeful grin. Suddenly I was struck with horror. I had lost my place! Panic gripped me as I scrambled to regain my position on the keys. I'm not sure if I was able to finish or not. I just knew that I had failed. And all for a smile.

My capacity for guilt was not limited to winning the approval of adults. My most painful childhood memories involve my younger sisters, Debby and Lindy.

I was strolling Debby in our driveway one day and she kept trying to stand up. My mothering instincts prompted a warning. "Debby! Don't stand up in the stroller! You could fall and get hurt!'' But she did stand up and fall and hurt herself. She landed on her head with a chilling thump. Although she healed nicely, thank God, my feelings of guilt didn't heal nearly as quickly. For years I felt totally responsible for her scarred forehead—as I did for Lindy's scarred hand.

One afternoon, to my horror, I saw Lindy running through the house with a knife and took it upon myself to protect her from harm. But as I quickly grabbed the knife from her hand, it sliced the fleshy web of skin that stretched between her thumb and forefinger. It was ages before I could bear to see her wound without experiencing a tremendous burden of guilt.

I never felt as badly about my own injuries as those of my sisters. In fact, when I bloodied my chin in a playground accident or split my eyelid in a ballet tumble, I wore the bandages like trophies. Somehow, I reveled in my victimization. I was actually proud of my pain. To me, "a kick was as good as a boost." Maybe even better. It seems crazy to me now, but I managed to turn things around so frequently. While I took pride in my sufferings, I never allowed myself to take full credit for my accomplishments.

On one paradoxical occasion, I made the newspapers for my "bravery" by awakening my family during an electrical fire that could have destroyed our house. It was all very exciting to a five-year-old—fire engines, screaming sirens, flashing lights. We even spent part of the night at the police station while firemen resolved the problem. I was treated like the heroine who saved the day. But I knew in my heart that I was scared to death when I'd noticed the night light wasn't working; I had groped my way, frightened of the darkness, to the maid's room to ask her to fix it. Sure, I had smelled something funny but I felt my prime motivation was fear, not heroism, and that everyone who praised me was making a mistake.

But those early years were not all fears and doubts for me. There were tender moments as well, like saying prayers at night, "God-blessing" everyone I could think of (to postpone climbing into bed, I think), including Lassie and Steve Allen. When Steve heard about it, he sent me an autographed picture that read, "God bless you, too, Cherry!" The funny moments were best—like getting a case of the giggles with my sisters at almost anything and sometimes at nothing at all.

I loved taking charge of the games we played with the throngs of neighborhood children. We would all congregate in our front yard for snowball fights, tag, pretending, and other games. In fact, I remember once being scolded for "taking charge" when we played "Three Stooges"; I was Moe and knocked the unassuming heads of Larry and Joe together with a crack! Curious. Larry and Joe never cried on television.

Television was a fascinating mystery to me. Especially when Daddy's show came on. I didn't understand how he could be sitting on the living room sofa while singing on the television screen at the same time. I finally solved the problem in a unique way. This was Daddy on the sofa with me, alive and warm and snuggling me with his strong, fatherly arms. And that was "Daddy Pat Boone" on the television—a two dimensional image made of glass, but somehow just as real as the father at my side. Daddy Pat Boone was like Santa Claus. He was someone *special*.

Faces lit up with excitement when people heard that *my* father was *the* Pat Boone—a handsome singer-star loved by the young generation and approved of (perhaps secretly admired) by their parents. In fact, I soon discovered that revealing my identity as Pat Boone's daughter changed the way people related to me. Suddenly I was a celebrity, too! Total strangers would make such a fuss over me that I eventually began to look for opportunities to spread the word: "You see Pat Boone over there? He's my Daddy. You want his autograph?"

What a ham! But that game was short-lived. A few spankings for bragging, making a spectacle of myself, and, of course, destroying my parents' attempts to maintain some degree of privacy quickly put an end to my attention-getting efforts. After all, I was much more interested in the approval of my mother and father than of people I didn't know.

As Daddy's career continued to soar, the time eventually came for the Boone family to trek westward to California. We had been crisscrossing the country with Daddy to do television shows in the East, films in the West. The move to Los Angeles became inevitable, with more and more show business activity originating from Hollywood. Pat Boone was now more than a singer and television celebrity; he was a full-fledged movie star.

This meant giving up the "Chevy Showroom," so plans were made for a farewell episode that would include the whole family—our first performance together. We were all excited about being on television with Daddy. We were to sing the final song with the whole cast! In the early stages of preparation, my dad asked if I would like to learn the words of a certain song and sing it myself on the show. Panic immediately swept through me as I thought of learning all those words, and singing them alone in front of all those people! What if I blew it like I had at my recital? What if I failed? At the same time I desperately wanted to please my dad, show him that I could meet the challenge, learn the song he wanted me to sing, and be the kind of person I thought he wanted me to be. Hesitatingly, I voiced my doubts. Daddy quickly responded that he would find someone else to do it if I couldn't handle it. "Maybe," he said, "we won't use the song at all."

What a dilemma! Either way, I would fall short. It was a double bind: I could take the challenge and make Daddy proud by trying to learn the song, but risked embarrassment and failure on a grand scale. Or, I could give in to my fears and avoid the risk all together, admitting my inability to live up to Daddy's expectations.

I didn't sing the song. But I did tell a joke and played my part with all the cuteness and confidence a five-year-old could muster. The show went well and I was relieved when I got a good laugh. With the final television episode behind us, the Pat Boone family packed up and blazed a trail from the Big Apple to Glitter City.

CHAPTER TWO

All That Glitters

Eternal sunshine. Wide, smoothly paved roads lined by gently swaying palms reaching skyward to explode like fireworks into sprays of many-fingered fronds rattling softly in the warm breeze. Beyond the trees stretched thick, green carpets of lawn, meticulously manicured, flanking long driveways adorned by shiny, well-polished Mercedes, BMWs, Cadillacs, Porsches, Rolls-Royces, and an exotic assortment of low-slung Italian sports cars. Their immaculately clean surfaces reflected images of multistoried mansions, protected by chains, gates, and wrought iron bars: the American dream.

Hollywood. Bel Air. Beverly Hills. The dwellings of celebrities, doctors, lawyers, corporate executives, agents, producers, and a variety of other show business and media elite peppered the area with splendid elegance. These are houses where neighbors often live next door to one another for the better part of a generation without any meaningful interaction—perhaps without even meeting unless by chance or through business. This was the atmosphere of affluence and apathy that was to become my home as a six-year-old observer of the Hollywood way of life.

In 1960 I was an outsider, there only by my relationship

to a newcomer on the scene. Little did I know that before the decade was done, I would be on the inside looking out. Nor did I imagine that this gilded frontier that had beckoned us westward would actually become the stage for a private and personal drama. How could I have known that a chain of events and influences would weave a deadly pattern around me; a web of woes more real and terrifying than anything produced by cameras, sets, or studios.

I remember the very moment when the six of us, with Daddy behind the wheel, rolled into the driveway of our new home to finally and officially move in. "This is going to be our 'haven of happiness,'" he announced.

This haven comprised more than an acre of land on a prominent corner in the very heart of Beverly Hills. A two-story white Colonial, the house was set like a jewel in the midst of lush, green, beautifully kept lawns and trimmed hedges surrounded by a knee-high white brick wall. In the backyard was the indispensable symbol of the truly successful southern Californian—a swimming pool. Of course, there were the appropriate accoutrements: expensive patio, pool houses, side yards, a greenhouse, and a small guest bungalow.

The house was comfortably furnished, creating a sense of warmth and casualness in contrast to the opulence of many Beverly Hills homes. There was a live-in maid, a resident babysitter, a cook, and a cleaning woman. My own room was decorated with a white canopy bed and ornate, French-style furniture. I felt like Cinderella just arrived at the ball. Impressive as our home was (and still is), some of our neighbors themselves could be considered even more spectacular: Edward G. Robinson, Ricardo Montalban, Larry "J. R. Ewing" Hagman, Carolyn Jones, Stan Freeberg, Don Adams, Doris Day, Lucille Ball, Jack

Benny, Jimmy Stewart, Dean Martin, Jimmy Durante—just to name a few—all lived within walking distance.

Our private school had star-studded PTA meetings with the likes of John Forsythe, John Kerr, Robert Taylor, Gregory Peck, Tony Curtis, Janet Leigh, Kirk Douglas, and Ronald Reagan in regular attendance. Of course I didn't know any better than to think that I was living a perfectly normal, average childhood with normal, average friends. Going to birthday parties at the homes of Debbie Reynolds and Jerry Lewis did not seem the least bit out of the ordinary.

Admittedly, there were those unforgettable occasions when I was awestruck by the presence of some supercelebrity—super, at least, in my opinion. At my seventh-birthday party, my parents arranged for the heartthrob of my young life to join us! From the then popular television series "77 Sunset Strip," Edd "Kookie" Byrnes came by to have cake and ice cream. As I remember, he presented me with one of his famous combs and a dictionary for translating his personal slang, "Kookie Talk," into understandable English. If I happened to have a mad crush on someone I would find myself, as if by magic, shaking hands with him. Meeting Will Hutchins from "Sugarfoot," David McCallum from "The Man from U.N.C.L.E.," Peter Brown from "The Rifleman," teen idols Bobby Sherman or Dean Martin, Jr., may not have seemed like much to anyone else but to me it was an opportunity to live out my wildest fantasies. I will never forget the day Elvis Presley stopped by our house for a visit, or the day my family and I went backstage after a concert at the Las Vegas Convention Center to meet John, Paul, George, and Ringo.

Eventually the novelty of Hollywood and its many trappings began to wear off. It became apparent that man cannot live by glitter alone, much of which is really only a glossy candy-coating to conceal a part of celebrity life that is bitter to the taste and difficult to swallow. The demands, the pressures, and the lack of privacy far outweigh the frills, I think. After a while you may awake to find that your life is not truly your own. You can be bought, sold, advertised, marketed, and merchandised like a piece of property, the hours of your schedule determined by others.

When our house was eventually added to the "movie-star map" hardly a day passed when autograph and picture seekers weren't ringing the doorbell or waiting by the driveway. Busloads of stargazers would spill out onto the sidewalk in front of our house clicking cameras and peering through windows. More than once we found total strangers standing at our back door or taking pictures of our swimming pool. Once, my sister Debby was unsuspectingly photographed through an open window—she was only half-clad at the time. Normal family outings became nearly impossible. On one trip to Disneyland, for example, my dad wore a disguise only to be recognized by a few incredibly persistent and observant fans. Eating an uninterrupted meal in a restaurant was a simple pleasure no longer to be enjoyed. But as things turned out, these were least on the list of inconveniences that are part of the price paid for fame and fortune.

There is an unwritten rule in show business, especially in the recording industry, which states that success is maintained by a lot of time "on the road." Unfortunately, my father was no exception. As I mentioned before, during one three-year period, he was away a year and a half! A particularly extensive tour which included a sweep of Africa took him from home for most of six months! In his protracted absences, my mother tried constantly to keep him in our minds, making him a part of our lives by creating a sense of his presence. "What do you think Daddy would say?" she often asked. In fact, Mommy buried herself in parenthood to compensate for our absentee Daddy. Her creative and personal touches are still fond memories, from our regular Saturday night shampoo and rub-down to our daily lunchbox surprise—a sandwich shaped with a different cookie cutter for each day of the week. Without Daddy there to carry me to my room and give me one of his golden goodnight kisses after I'd fallen asleep on their king-sized bed, I often got to spend the whole night with Mommy. We kept each other company—I represented a part of Daddy to her, and sharing that big bed with her represented security to me.

When he was home, Daddy kept busy with television appearances, recording, and movie making. He did guest shots on several variety shows and made frequent rounds on the talk show circuit. He even hosted a couple of interview programs of his own. More hit records kept Daddy on the pop charts, "Moody River" and "Speedy Gonzales" being among them. He starred in films like "All Hands on Deck" and "State Fair" and played a small role in "The Greatest Story Ever Told" as the angel in the empty tomb.

There were a few other movies made during that period but their popularity at the box office left something to be desired. In fact, Twentieth Century-Fox executives were getting a bit nervous. They decided it was time to change Pat Boone's image from "Mr. Goodie White Shoes" to a tough, young sex symbol in order to compete with current Hollywood fare.

In January 1963, Daddy was sent to England to film "The Main Attraction," a movie the moguls had chosen specifically to turn the old Pat Boone into the new James Dean,

complete with leather jacket, cigarettes, and an obvious air
of rebellious restlessness. It was scheduled for three months
of production, so the whole family accompanied him to
avoid another lengthy separation.

During our stay in a London suburb, my mother entered
the hospital without so much as a word to us regarding her
illness. It was not until many years later that I learned of her
miscarriage. The pregnancy was never announced to us.
Undoubtedly my parents had their reasons for concealing
the matter; however, I must confess a deep sense of
disappointment at being left out of such a vital family
development.

Furthermore, such secrecy was not confined to the
miscarriage. It seemed as if there were several strategic,
topical taboos: family financial matters were such an issue.
On a few occasions I recall my dad mentioning money at the
dinner table only to be met by my mother's urgent
"shushing" or a head-spinning change of subject. They
would not allow us to get the impression that money was
always plentiful and easy to come by. Of course, they
viewed this as a protective measure.

Money was not the only subject cloistered in the privacy
of my parents' room. Although the specifics were difficult
to determine through closed doors, it was certainly apparent
that loud and emotional outbursts were growing in both
frequency and intensity. To say that Mommy and Daddy
weren't getting along too well would be putting it mildly.
The Hollywood lifestyle was taking a tremendous toll on
their seemingly ideal marriage and while my dad could keep
his problems hidden beneath a cool exterior, my mom
erupted when the pressure became too great. On more than
one occasion she bolted in a huff to one of the cars for a fast,
angry drive to blow off steam. I can still remember the

screeching tires and the unanswered questions hanging in the air.

The conflicts reached such a crescendo that all love and life appeared to be drained from their relationship, leaving a passionless partnership where a marriage had once been. We girls were protected, of course, from the details of these conflicts. We didn't know what they were, how they developed, or why they weren't being resolved. One thing we did know was that the full weight of the situation came crashing down on Mom, landing her in a hospital bed with a severe case of what was thought to be mononucleosis. She lost twenty pounds in twelve days and, as she now asserts, could have died. But she made a desperate, conscious effort to survive and came home on her birthday. In light of the multiple crises facing our family, it seemed a miracle that she opted for life.

My parents' marriage had been undermined by the influences of Hollywood and, as if this wasn't depressing enough, the dream of never-ending superstardom was headed for the rocks as well. Fame is fickle and often fades as rapidly as it appears. Just as the mirage of water in the desert turns to sand in the fingers of a thirsty man, the hit record or smash film can disappear into tremendously frustrating illusions, urgently sought but just barely out of reach. It looked as though Pat Boone had ridden the crest of his career and now the wave of public opinion was ebbing.

Daddy felt his career was being threatened and as he scrambled to secure his footing on the mountaintop of success, the specter of financial ruin crept up on us from behind. Poor business advice led to bad investments that, when compounded by lower income from fewer hit records and movies, led us to the brink of bankruptcy. For a time, foreclosure on our Beverly Hills house seemed inevitable.

The tremors that jolted our household could have rivaled any California earthquake but, in spite of this, the image we maintained was one of happiness and stability. Even we girls were not fully aware of the problems and their devastating ramifications. After all, we were people in the public eye and were expected to be flawless.

The public has an oddly conflicting set of expectations and standards by which to judge its heroes. When it came to the Boones, the public seemed cross-eyed. Secular audiences had a very specific idea of what Pat Boone (and family) should be, seeing him as a Hollywood star. But this same Pat Boone was also an outspoken, widely published Christian leader, and his church following had quite another idea. Being Pat Boone's daughter was very much like being a celebrity's kid and a preacher's kid all at the same time: maintaining the Boone image was like balancing on a tightrope.

My parents had made a decision early in their lives: it was better to be too strict than too lenient, and strict they were. After all, raising children in the modern world was challenging enough, but raising four pretty little girls to be unspoiled Christian young women while living in a show-business environment was like a family version of "Mission Impossible." Consequently, there were seemingly endless rules and regulations regarding where we went, with whom, for how long, movies we saw, television programs we watched, clothes, hair lengths, bedtimes, dating, and makeup. My mom and dad were really only trying to make life easier for us, to do their best for the good of the family. Despite the goodness and purity of their motives, however, even they now admit in retrospect that they were overprotective.

I considered the policies laid down by my parents to be

solemn, binding law written, as it were, on tablets of stone. I knew disobedience would result in swift, sure punishment. For the most part I was compliant, so spankings were relatively infrequent. I was strangely thankful for the uncommon spanking I *did* receive because it created a kind of penitential release for me—a victory over the nagging, inner torment of guilt. There would be a time of praying, crying, and hugging after the punishment and this seemed to give me a new lease on life.

Somehow it never occurred to me to question the rules or the rule makers until the infamous makeup restriction. This edict dictated that no cosmetics were to be used before the age of thirteen. By twelve years of age I looked more like fifteen and had grown to five feet four inches. My friends were older and I naturally wanted to be accepted as a peer. Makeup was a part of this and, as it turned out, my first significant point of defiance on the home front. Confrontations with Daddy were frequent and severe. He referred to my supply of cosmetics as "war paint."

The opening skirmish of a long battle began one sunny Sunday morning as the family headed out of the driveway for church. My dad made a passing glance at me in the rearview mirror and suddenly hit the brakes.

"What is that on your face, young lady?"

"Who, me? Nothing. Why do you . . ." I was cut off before I could finish my question.

"Don't you lie to me! Get upstairs right now and wash your face."

"But, Daddy!"

"Don't you 'but Daddy' me! I've told you repeatedly about this and we are not going to leave until you go wash your face. Now make it snappy—we're already late!"

I went up to my room and, with a damp cloth, tried to

blend in the foundation and make it appear completely natural. The attempts to camouflage my artistry backfired and I received a spanking. That same afternoon I emerged from the house to watch some neighborhood boys playing basketball. With incredible boldness, I had frosted my lips and lightened the puffy circles under my eyes. Even Laury, the mischief-making expert in our family, beheld me in wide-eyed disbelief.

The era of problem-free parent-child relations had become a thing of the past. For the first time I was challenging my parents. I may have looked older than many of my friends but my parents were determined to keep me from "growing up too fast." They even withdrew me from school after completing the sixth grade with straight A's to repeat the same grade in a new setting—a private girls' school (I had skipped the second grade so they wanted to place me back with my own age group).

Regardless of parental efforts to cool my grasping for maturity, Mother Nature's biological clock would not be stopped. Almost thirteen, I felt like a child in my white bobby socks and patent-leather pumps while two years earlier, on my eleventh birthday, I had received the "curse" of womanhood. It was for me a truly baffling experience in emotional contradiction—feeling so adult and so hopelessly juvenile at the same time. Physically I was becoming a woman while my parents continued to regard me as a child. They were bound to keep me that way until they felt I was ready to be responsible for my own life. Besides, I had to set the example for my three younger sisters, who would be following in my footsteps, and although I might be mature enough to handle certain responsibilities, the other girls might not be. So for consistency's sake, the rules remained fixed for all of us equally. I can't count the times that Daddy would negatively respond to my requests to go somewhere or do something beyond our predetermined limits with the statement, "It's not that we don't trust *you*. We just don't thrust the devil and we don't trust human nature!" As far as I was concerned, that meant they didn't trust me.

Compared to the crucial issues plaguing our family at this juncture, my personal struggles were relatively inconsequential. However, there is no doubt in my mind that these traumas combined to create a pervasive inner sensation of helplessness and the feeling that my life was something over which I had little or no control. My entire world was being shaken—my images of marriage, family, career, and finances; my relationship with my parents, and, finally, my own personal identity. Everything seemed transitory and uncertain.

Underneath the smiling surface, the joyful substance of carefree childhood was wasting away. A storm was brewing inside and before too long, the glossy, candy-coated Cherry who reflected the surrounding Hollywood fairyland would wither and cave in on herself.

CHAPTER THREE

A Recipe for Self-Destruction

Any tempest eventually comes to an end, no matter how wild or lengthy, or how great the damage left in its wake. After several torrential years, the Boone family began to breathe a sigh of relief as the black clouds separated to reveal patches of blue over our Beverly Hills home once more.

When my parents reached the end of their rope in a sea of financial worries, their last hope for salvation was spiritual. First my mother and then my father recommitted themselves to a faith in God that had once been a lively flame giving them purpose and direction, but that had been reduced by the cares of their world to a barely smoldering ember. This dynamic experience created new levels of strength and enthusiasm that had never been a part of their previous religious experience. They reevaluated their priorities as Christians, realizing that in nurturing their inner life, their day-to-day challenges could be met with a new perspective and resolved with God's help.

This spiritual renewal affected nearly all areas of our lives, transforming in Midas-like fashion almost everything it was allowed to touch. My parents' marriage began to show signs of new life, like the first leaves of spring after a long, cold winter. And when my dad began to relinquish his desperate pursuit of career and financial success, things began to fall into place with considerably less effort—like the elusive butterfly that lands on one's shoulder once the net has been put away.

To a teenager facing the transformation that Father Time and Mother Nature inevitably work within us all, the prospect of stability was most welcome—like a reprieve from another impending storm. Daddy's presence became critical for my sisters and me; a strong male role model was necessary as we approached the dating years. So when the opportunity arose for Daddy's solo show to become a traveling sextet, the Pat Boone Family Act was born. The perfect way for a protective father to keep his growing chicks beneath his safe, strong, and very strict wings proved a surprising financial success.

Performing with our father happened almost by accident. We had always sung together at home and at church—with musical talent on both sides of the family it was a natural. But now my dad was asked to tour Japan with a budding new family group, then achieving only limited success in the United States. The Japanese tour coordinator commented on the oriental emphasis upon the family and suggested that Daddy bring us along. When Daddy informed Mr. Nagashima that we girls did a little singing of our own, his eyes sparkled with delight.

"The fan magazines in Tokyo already refer to you as their hometown boy, Pat. They love you so much they even retouch your photographs to give you oriental eyes! Seeing Shirley and the girls would be like welcoming family!"

So began my show business career at age fourteen with a concert tour of Japan in the spring of 1969. The Pat Boone Family and the Osmond Family were a winning combination to the oriental audiences. We girls took to the experience like fish to water. We loved singing, dancing, being on stage, receiving the warm appreciation of the Japanese, and being treated with the unparalleled hospitality of the East. Of course we also enjoyed traveling with the Osmonds. There was at least one Osmond brother for each Boone girl and we paired off according to age, on stage and off. They were an inspiration to us as new performers and became close friends for years to come.

What began as a one-time experiment mushroomed into full-blown show-business involvement. Back home, we began to appear regularly with Daddy on major television shows (with Flip Wilson, Glen Campbell, Merv Griffin, Mike Douglas, Dinah Shore, and on the "Tonight Show"), as well as doing national and international concert tours and performing in showrooms and night clubs. We broke the attendance record during our one-month stay at a downtown Las Vegas hotel. Local television interview shows in major cities became routine and we appeared on a few network television specials with Perry Como, John Wayne, Elizabeth Taylor, Paul Newman, Henry Fonda, Charley Pride, Cheryl Ladd, Henry Mancini, and other notables. We rode in parades, sold an array of products on television, and sang at conventions.

A personal highlight was leading the Pledge of Allegiance at the 1972 Republican convention and performing for the president and other heads of state at his second inaugural gala. We met with Richard Nixon in the Oval Office privately, then entertained him at the Kennedy Center along with Frank Sinatra, Bob Hope, Sammy Davis, Jr., and several other top stars. A reception followed and I found myself in the company of Secretary of State Henry Kissinger. The following day I attended the official inaugural dinner with young Richard Nixon, the president's nephew and namesake. All of this because of one persistent Japanese booking agent!

We were now fully initiated into the inner circle of Hollywood's "chosen people." What more could a teenage girl want out of life than to be a part of the world that most folks only dream about; hobnobbing with the superstars and traveling the globe. But while it provided thrills and excitement, it also presented many challenges to both my sisters and me that most young girls never know. We took our roles as performers seriously and worked diligently at them. At the same time our parents warned us that if school work suffered, it would be "bye-bye show biz." Although most of our performances were scheduled during the summer, it was not unusual to spend one week each month on the road during the school year.

I had always been a perfectionist and this carried over into my performing. But my schoolwork, too, had been of the utmost importance to me from the moment I walked into my first classroom. Straight A's were my uncompromising objective. I knew I was capable of them and I wouldn't settle for less. In the fourth grade I would stay up until eleven o'clock to put the finishing touches on my homework. The mere thought of falling below my personal scholastic standards flooded me with panic. It's not difficult to imagine the mortification I felt when I once received a glaring red F for a math test on material covered in my absence.

Exams struck fear in my heart so I often feigned illness to escape them, compiling a long record of missed school days. My consistently perfect grades were based on weekly work loads maintained with tedious attention to detail. When confronted with the possibility of falling short of my own unrealistically high expectations, I opted to avoid the challenge completely.

I was transferred from my first school, John Thomas Dye (a coeducational private school), to Westlake School for Girls after having finished the sixth grade. The all-girl environment was a welcome change after having been the brunt of constant teasing and harassment by the boys at John Thomas Dye. I repeated grade six at Westlake, continuing a flawless flow of report cards until I reached the eighth grade and had to study Chinese history. It seemed like a horrendous waste of time and energy. I'm not sure if I wasn't doing well in the class because I disliked it, or if I disliked it because I wasn't gliding effortlessly through it. Regardless, I began to wake up "feeling sick" frequently.

I knew I couldn't fake illness indefinitely so I tried to find ways to convince my parents that I was legitimately ill. I went through my mother's medicine chest, grabbing any pill that looked like it might alter my physical condition enough to back up my story: sleeping pills, diet pills, antibiotics, laxatives. I would report that I had vomited after meals, conveniently flushing the toilet before anyone could verify my story. It worked for a while. But one day I was confronted by our housekeeper, who had a feeling I was pulling the wool over everyone's eyes.

"You ain't sick," she said. "Anybody can throw up—all you gotta do is stick your finger down your throat!"

A new idea! How much more convincing it would be if I really did throw up and had the evidence to prove it! So, to avoid being overwhelmed by Miss Piggott's Chinese history class, I missed forty days of school that year, was allowed to drop the class at the request of my parents, and take the rest of my finals at home. Ultimately I managed to keep my straight-A record unblemished and my extremely fragile sense of self-worth intact.

Academic striving was nothing new to me. There were, however, new concerns emerging from our growing show-business involvement. For a performer, physical appearance becomes of primary importance. Self-consciousness is inevitable when you are constantly being stared at on stage or scrutinized in a fan magazine. Suddenly, every imperfection, real or imagined, is a focal point for alteration and improvement. Having developed early and grown more rapidly than the average girl, the excess "baby fat" that I retained looked out of place. I had become self-conscious about my size by age thirteen. And when an eighteen-year-old male friend of our family commented on the value of thinness, I began dieting immediately.

"Thin is in, you know!" he said. "Skinny legs are outa sight! You can never be too thin or too rich."

I joined the "Metrecal-for-lunch bunch," freezing my dietetic chocolate liquid to eat like ice cream at school. At night I would empty a can containing a "Metrecal meal" into a bowl and slowly savor my supper substitute. My special food created some jealousy in Lindy, who, when told emphatically she could not go on a diet, promptly went on a weight-gaining campaign so that she could then join me in my abstinence.

My weight loss and exercise programs were successful, but somehow not enough. On one of my eighth-grade medicine-chest raids, I happened upon a prescription labeled Eskatrol. With laxatives I had experienced hyper-activity, but these colorful little capsules brought me boundless energy and euphoria. They were diet pills prescribed to my mother.

My accidental discovery of diet pills was the beginning of

another power struggle. For me those multicolored capsules were also multipurpose: they made me feel as if I could accomplish anything, they gave me an extra charge of energy for exercising, they suppressed any thought of food, and they helped me produce some top-notch term papers.

It wasn't unusual for me to take one at bedtime and then work on a project all night long. The only problem was that after a while my tolerance to them increased, forcing me to double my dosage to get the desired effect. As the pills disappeared, my mother had to call for refills more often. Eventually, in order to avoid being caught, I called the pharmacist myself pretending to be Mrs. Boone. I would then walk to the drugstore posing as my mother (confident in my mature appearance) to pick up the prescription. Eventually the doctor realized that excessive dosages were being ordered and he notified my mother. Her surprise at his warning indicated that something was amiss.

She once saw a few of the capsules fall out of my pocket and told me not to take any more of them. But I was already becoming dependent on them and ignored her request. When the pills continued to disappear, my parents confronted me about my deliberate disobedience. I denied everything, but they knew that I was responsible so they hid the bottle. Being a skillful detective I found the pills and took as many as I felt I could get away with. When the risk became too great, I resorted to my drugstore scheme. That was when the doctor called. My parents didn't have to look far to find the culprit. My addiction and the lengths to which I would go to feed it were enough to force my mother to cancel the prescription. When my mother found my secret stash that was to last me through an entire month in Las Vegas, she confiscated it. With that, neither of us had another capsule of Eskatrol—and both of us ballooned in weight.

After having become accustomed to a lean 113 pounds, within six months I tilted the scales at a solid 140!

Curiously, even with the head-on collisions with my parents, my relationship with them was excessively close. I shared almost everything openly: my anxieties regarding schoolwork, my weight and general feelings of failure, and my growing interest in the opposite sex. I was experiencing the natural adolescent excitement and curiosity about this newly developing dimension of my life, and beginning to attract the attention of young men (including that eighteen-year-old family friend). My parents discouraged physical involvement and encouraged group activities. "Be careful and prayerful," Daddy carefully admonished as we left with our dates.

Since puberty had rushed upon me early, our pediatrician advised my mother to "have a talk" with me when I was nine. All I remember of that conversation was reading a book about hamsters. As I approached adolescence, my mother often stressed the sacredness my first kiss should and would have with the right person. I was painfully disappointed when, in the summer of 1968, a stray hippie we had taken in overnight stole my precious first kiss from me. In tears I informed Mommy. After we prayed and cried together, my dad confronted (and evicted) our long-haired houseguest.

My first voluntary encounter occurred several months later with none other than the young man so fond of skinny legs. Thus began a two-year relationship that was, for the most part, promoted by my parents, as long as we were in constant view of their watchful, protective eyes. For a while all went well, but after he joined the navy his rare visits home proved more than this inexperienced, impressionable fifteen-year-old could handle. By that time my boyfriend was twenty years old and expected a certain degree of physical interaction in our relationship. On one occasion, with my father out of town and my mother asleep in the same room, he used his physical strength to force activities in which I didn't want to share. Although I never lost my virginity, his sexual intimidation reached a level that made me uneasy in the following months. I felt secretive, deceptive, and even tainted by the ongoing involvement. Overwhelming guilt and an undefined fear overtook me. Eventually, unable to cope any longer, I severed the relationship. I ended up sharing with my mother the reasons for the breakup and how it had all started that night in her bedroom. She agreed that I had made the right decision and, with great remorse over her unknowing complicity, decided it would remain our secret. Daddy wouldn't have to know about it. After this, any sexual involvement beyond the most innocent of kisses produced anxiety and alarm.

The closeness I experienced with my parents seemed such a harbor of safety to me and such a pleasing thing to them that when my siblings showed any reticence to be as communicative as I was, I would intervene with the counsel of a sister older and wiser in the ways of family diplomacy. It was not uncommon for me to act as peacemaker in situations of conflict between my parents and the girls. I often found myself in the middle of a squabble pleading my parents' love and good intentions to one of my sisters and explaining to my mother or father why she was behaving inappropriately. I remember the satisfaction I felt when such counseling sessions served as steps towards understanding and reconciliation between a distraught parent and a very rebellious daughter.

At one point Debby had become the primary focus for parental concern. She was starting to succumb to the typical peer pressure of preadolescence. The result was an unkempt, denim-clad hard rocker with glaring eyes that projected hatred towards anything or anyone that smacked of authority. With her rebellious attitude and rigid ideas, she was attempting to make her own personal declaration of independence. She even tacked her non-conformity to her bedroom walls in the form of psychedelic posters of Jimi Hendrix and the original "Easy Riders."

My efforts as family mediator were much appreciated by my parents, whose battle fatigue was beginning to show. I may not have been responsible for a peace settlement but at least I was able to establish a cease-fire and both parties seemed satisfied with the outcome. I pleased everyone and came out the "hero" with both parental and sibling approval as my trophies. Since Lindy was always the carefree, untroubled Boone girl, and because Laury's behavioral aberrations were more mischievous than malicious, harmony in our Hollywood home seemed to be a reality. Our image as the ideal American family was salvaged once again.

This smooth sailing was largely due to the fact that each of us girls had begun to experience the same kind of spiritual renewal as had Mommy and Daddy. Our personal commitments to our faith kept the usual overt sibling rivalry at bay (although I must admit that my inner desire to excel and be preeminent never waned). In fact, when several tragedies threatened to rock the boat, this newly developed dependence on God that we all held in common helped keep us afloat. Similar events taking place prior to our spiritual rededication would have certainly dashed us against the rocks. When our maid of many years (who had also been the housekeeper in my mother's home when she was growing up) died of lung cancer, my mom was devastated. Her severe reaction disturbed me. My own regrets were based on my stormy relationship with the maid; her death evoked my guilt.

In sharp contrast, shortly after the seeds of spiritual serenity had taken root, my grandfather Red Foley died unexpectedly in his middle 50s. I had last seen him on my fourteenth birthday when he ws performing at Disneyland. Only two months later he passed away in his sleep in Fort Wayne, Indiana, while on a concert tour. My mother was delivering a speech at a home for delinquent boys when our babysitter reported that Daddy Red had died.

Hot tears spilled onto my flushed cheeks as I thought of the effect this would have on Mommy. Because his death would make the news, I had the babysitter drive me to the McCobb Home for Boys so that we could catch my mom before she got in her car to drive home—letting her hear it announced on the radio would have been a ruthless blow. When I saw her emerge from the building with Bob McCobb, I got out of the car and met her in front of her Cadillac.

"What are you doing here, honey?" she asked with surprise. I looked up at her sadly and then down at the street as I fought to maintain my composure.

"It's Daddy Red, Mommy . . . he's gone."

She leaned back against her car and took a long, deep breath. Then to my amazement she put her hands on my face and looked into my eyes saying, "The Lord hasn't brought us this far to let us down now, Cherry. Daddy Red's with Jesus and the Lord will give us the strength we need to go on." He did—so much so that Mommy wore a peaceful smile through the entire funeral.

Her example of steadfastness in the face of personal trauma was timely indeed; shortly after her father's passing, my best friend died following efforts to remove a malignant brain tumor. She was fourteen years old. I visited her in the hospital just before the operation to let her know we were praying for her. The next week in a school assembly, after successful surgery and positive signs of recovery, our headmaster announced that Wendy's heart had suddenly stopped. A shock wave jolted all in the auditorium. Debby, who was sitting next to me, recoiled at the news; her intense reaction produced a nosebleed. I slumped back in my chair and whispered, "Lord, help me!" Not a tear was shed. A few days later I delivered the eulogy at her funeral.

The month before Wendy's death, my dad's grandfather passed away. All of us were sorry to see Granddaddy Pritchard go. He had always been one of the highlights of our trips to Jacksonville, Florida, where we often visited relatives. His distinctive, deep hearty chuckle, along with the humorous Brer Rabbit stories that he serialized from visit to visit, are still dear memories.

The deaths of loved ones were times of bereavement for me, but somehow I did not enter into the grief process. I thought I was being strong—in control—by maintaining my composure. My apparent strength was probably an unconscious escape mechanism from facing the cold realities of death and loss.

In spite of the challenges faced by the Boones, an atmosphere of relative calm ensued. The fortress of family stability, once under direct siege by a company of hostile influences, stood unshaken. Ironically, this calm was actually the eye in the center of a raging hurricane that lulled us into believing the worst was behind. There could be no real way of knowing then that these events, traumas, and changes were the ingredients of a toxic recipe, unwittingly mixed together in a potion to create a monster that would ravage us all.

As I reflect on these events, I can now see a sequence of developments weaving a silent inner network of terror—a terror that would infiltrate and gradually overtake me. The individual components alone probably would not have led to such a nightmare but together they created disaster: family instability, financial stress, my father's absences, high expectations, high visibility, perfectionism, over-protection, confused sexual identity accompanied by fear of womanhood and adult responsibilities, dread of the mere thought of sexual involvement, excessive dieting and exercise, sibling rivalry, my perceived role as mediator between family members, and unresolved grief. Here was a formula for self-destruction.

CHAPTER FOUR

Fat, Fear, and Frenzy

Quietly I opened my closet door, wincing with each whine of the hinges. I tugged on the cord attached to the bare light bulb on the ceiling. While dressing quickly I gathered a few overnight things, gave my bedroom one more check for any last minute necessities, then slipped into the hall. I stepped carefully so as not to wake anyone with the creaking of the wooden stairs, and descended stealthily into the shadowy darkness. I tiptoed past the maid's room, secured the keys to the family station wagon, and carefully unlocked the back door's double bolt.

Once outside I released the breath I'd held, exhaling a steam cloud into the cool, starlit sky. The maid's window was right next to the car; I had to continue to move with caution, praying she would not be awakened by the engine rumbling to life. While turning the key in the ignition I gave a quick punch to the accelerator and waited to see if any lights switched on to pierce the inky blackness of the slumbering household . . . nothing. The family Ford slowly rolled out of the driveway and into the unknown, like a magic carpet flying me to uncharted territory and unexperienced freedoms.

This wasn't the first covert ride on my own personal

midnight express—I had taken other nighttime drives in several of our cars. The reason these joy rides were always timed for the wee hours of the morning was simple: I was fifteen and had only a learner's permit; my license would have to wait until after my sixteenth birthday. Yes, it was illegal and yes, I realized I would be in deep trouble if apprehended, but I was more concerned about the consequences of discovery by my parents than by the police. And my main misgiving about being caught by the California highway patrol was how it would reflect on my family and how they might react. The legal consequences of my actions somehow escaped me. I just enjoyed the liberty, the speed, and the exhilarating, adult feeling of being out on my own piloting my freedom machine through miles of empty Los Angeles streets. It was my own special secret.

This particular night was different, however. I was not intending to return by dawn as was my usual strategy.

After the breakup with my first serious boyfriend I rebounded into a very brief friendship with a fellow even older than the first. I backed out immediately when the emotional and physical dimensions of the relationship intensified, frightening me into slamming the brakes on relationship number two.

Moreover, as our family act became more popular, keeping up with schoolwork was becoming a real challenge; my life was slipping more and more out of my control. It seemed that I was being constantly dictated to by people and circumstances—expectations from the secular and Christian publics along with my role as dutiful daughter and exemplary older sister were closing in on me. I felt like a helpless victim in a horror movie where the walls suddenly begin to move towards the center of the room.

This claustrophobic atmosphere had brought me to a

decision: I had to break away from these pressures and spend a few days in solitude. I felt the need to pray, to think, to sort out my increasingly complicated life. So I embarked on what I had planned to be a retreat of sorts—to get in touch with God and, with His help and guidance, to make some choices of my own.

Once I had traveled beyond the reach of parental "radar," my plans somehow took on a novel twist. I realized that I had taken my life into my own hands. I had seized the initiative and was free to do anything I desired. I was immediately bombarded with a myriad of temptations to participate in activities my super-ego would normally have regarded as "anathema." It was like opening Pandora's box: here was my chance to sample a smorgasbord of "no-nos" in that ominous, threatening world from which my parents were so solicitously protecting me. After all, how could I fully appreciate the value of good without experiencing a few of life's supposed evils. Once the customary restraints were removed, my imagination generated wild thoughts of experimentation with drugs and, ironically, with sex. Visions of sleeping on the beach, visiting discotheques, and other impossible dreams drew me further into my runaway fantasies.

Then, as if rewinding a tape, all of the demons that taunted me flew like fluttering bats back to their dark dwelling place. I came to my senses.

"Where am I going? What am I doing?" I asked myself in a sudden, sobering moment. "I could get myself killed!"

A deep dread subdued me with the realization of what lay hidden in the inner recesses of my psyche, and just how close I had come to making some irreversible mistakes. Still, I refused to go back home. On the one hand, I needed to be on my own. But on the other, I wanted to be safe (maybe from myself). So I drove to the home of the Osmond family, whom we hadn't seen for months, and parked in front of their house. I locked the doors, stretched out in the back of the station wagon, and dozed off for what remained of the night.

Although I had resisted the previous evening's temptations, the choice of my ultimate destination was not as innocent as it may have seemed. The recent lack of contact between the Boones and the Osmonds had been at least partly the result of my parents' concern about what we perceived to be attempts to proselytize us towards their own faith, which was quite different from ours. Any social activities would have to be initiated by them, my parents said, or there would be none at all. It seemed to me that this kind of approach was not fair. They deserved some kind of explanation and this was my chance to give it to them. Perhaps this was as far as my conscience would allow me to go with my daring exercise in self-assertion.

I stayed with the Osmonds for two days, after which time Mrs. Osmond called my parents to reassure them. I shared with the Osmonds the cause of the Boone family's silence. I felt I had restored the strained interfamily relationship, while successfully escaping, if only briefly, the pressure cooker that was my life. I had not, however, resolved any major issues or come to any dramatic decisions. I'd hardly prayed. My big retreat had become a mere weekend vacation.

Of course my mom and dad were frantic with worry over my disappearance, and at the same time half afraid of finding me. During my two-day absence their imaginations flooded them with horrible images every time they heard a siren or watched the current television news reports of people murdered in campers by the roadside! When I finally contacted them, I maintained a cool, matter-of-fact tone of voice as I divulged the details of my escapade. I drove home that evening to an emotional welcome; the obligatory chastisement was scaled down to my tremendous relief. The incident was devastating to my parents but for me it was an incredibly daring adventure, an attempt to do something on my own with ostensibly noble motives. It really represented my escalating desire for some kind of basic personal independence. I wanted to fly like an emancipated bird from my gilded cage.

Meanwhile, a new relationship began to develop "in the wings"—literally. I had known Warren, a member of another show business family, and of another religion, for a few years already, but only as a friend. In spite of the theological barriers, our friendship was now blossoming into a refreshingly unthreatening teenage romance. Of course, much of this depth was developed by correspondence—we had to maintain one of those long-distance loves if there was to be any at all because both of us spent so much time on the road. By chance, we occasionally ended up in the same place at the same time for an extended period—in fact, that is how the stage was set for our first date, my very first ever.

Our family was renting a house in Las Vegas for one month in the summer of 1970 while we performed two shows a night at the Fremont Hotel. I was thrilled to learn that Warren's family would be coming in to support Andy Williams at Caesars Palace before we were scheduled to depart. Because of religious discrepancies, diplomatic relations had not been fully established between the families. When we met them unexpectedly at the Las Vegas airport, I was ecstatic. There was no graceful way out; we would have to see them while we were all in town.

See them we did. In fact, that summer saw the development of our family friendship. It also brought my sixteenth birthday—my "legal" dating age! I wasn't about to let it slip by without cashing in on my long-promised privilege.

My lifestyle was already out of the ordinary. None of my teenage girlfriends would be spending a part of their summer in Phyllis Diller's rental home. Nor would they retire at three o'clock in the morning after a day (which started at half-past seven) of sunning, swimming, dieting, doing correspondence courses, going to the health club for a workout, and doing two strenuous shows each night for packed houses. Certainly none of them would have their birthday celebrated in a Las Vegas showroom and then proceed to another top hotel for their first date with one of its headliners.

Warren and I left Caesars Palace at one o'clock in the morning for dinner, after which he hailed a cab and delivered me to my doorstep at four. Even then it seemed extremely confusing to me that my protective parents would have allowed such a flagrant bending of the rules. Normally curfew would have been at eleven, and then only with a complete rundown of our itinerary given before departure. Furthermore, downtown Las Vegas would hardly have been their first choice for a dating locale. However, this was just one of several inconsistencies that I welcomed at the time. Only later would the conflicting messages I received from them have perplexing effects.

That month in Las Vegas was the occasion for another life-altering first. Shortly after our arrival, my mother discovered my stolen diet pills and dumped them down the toilet. Without the pills my discipline had to be strengthened considerably. I'd become accustomed to an occasional food binge followed by the ingestion of Eskatrol to burn the midnight oil and enough calories to undo the damage I had done. Once my dietary crutches were kicked out from under me I set out with single-minded determination to design a rigid regimen to ensure myself against gorging. But my willpower was gradually fading.

For my birthday I was presented with a lucious white cake with strawberry filling covered with the creamiest of frostings—one of my chronic weaknesses. After our first performance I had a small slice but when the second show was over, much of the sweet surprise remained uneaten. After a brief battle with my resolve to avoid such culinary entrapment, I reasoned that it was my birthday cake after all, and it should definitely not go to waste. My initial nibbling at crumbs graduated to uncontrolled feasting on globs of icing until eventually the platter's contents looked like a condemned building.

With a bloated belly and a crushed conscience, I rode back to the house in silence with the rest of the family. Once we retired to our rooms I began to prepare for bed, attempting to ignore my abdominal discomfort. Suddenly I recalled the trick I employed to avoid my eighth-grade history class—self-induced vomiting. It was at once revolting yet inevitable, as if I had no choice. I could stick my fingers down my throat and rid myself of the consequences of my gluttony.

As I prepared for the once-familiar ritual, another inner struggle was taking place. I had promised myself, and God, that I would never force myself to throw up again. I had successfully kept that promise from that moment until now. My full stomach ached for relief and the guilt I felt for my gluttony outweighed the remorse I anticipated for breaking my commitment. Slowly, deliberately, and with some regret, I proceeded to disgorge. When it was all over I went to bed feeling a little numb, partly from the shock of soaring blood sugar and electrolyte imbalance and partly from my nagging guilt. I was literally able to have my cake and eat it, too! But I resolved never to repeat the incident. As I drifted off to sleep I reassured myself that it would not happen again.

That birthday binge inaugurated a pattern of intemperance. The loss of my diet pills and self-discipline unleashed a seemingly insatiable appetite and my eating went virtually unchecked. It was as if my self-control had been an elastic band stretched to capacity when almost without warning it snapped! The tension was too much and, having reached its limits, my tightly strung resolutions went suddenly flaccid. By the winter of 1970–71, my weight had skyrocketed to 140 pounds. As if that was not debilitating enough to a delicate ego so absorbed with image, our public appearances on stage and television were becoming more frequent and more significant. I did my best to conceal the excess padding but my fat could not have been a secret to an observant viewer.

Still my intake was unrestrained. Every day in the early afternoon I routinely ate a bowl of granola cereal and cream while curling up in an upholstered armchair to watch "The Galloping Gourmet," jotting down his elaborate recipes between calorie-packed bites.

I had completely stopped exercising, even dropping my promising tennis game. My lessons were terminated due to our travels and when I attempted to resume my game it had drastically deteriorated. True to form, I gave up tennis rather than play with the frustration of knowing it was less than my maximum ability.

The dreaded day for our annual school photographs

arrived and I donned my uniform as always. For the first time I noticed that my white blouse was so snug around my hips that I could not fasten the last button. Fortunately, I thought, it would not show when tucked into my skirt, but I panicked when I tried to zip my skirt and the zipper refused to budge. Buttoning the waistband also proved a lost cause. Obviously self-conscious, I was primping in the girls' room before being summoned by the photographer when a friend commented on my expanding proportions. Just a few days before, one of Debby's friends had laughed with incredulity at the width of my hips.

The painful truth was unavoidable, and after enduring the ordeal of my class portrait that afternoon I waited in the driveway for my ride home. A surprising and terrible realization seized me as I stared down at my legs—when I stood with my feet together, they touched from my knees all the way up, but there was no point of contact from my knees down. I spread my feet a few inches and to my abject horror the result was the same. Everything from my knees up was still touching! Tears filled my eyes and desperate thoughts filled my mind as I sat on the curb in complete and utter despondence.

I went home, my spirit shattered, and cried all afternoon. When my sisters questioned the cause of my depression, I blurted out, "I'm as fat as Connie Sampson!" (She was the heaviest girl in our school.) "I hate myself!" I continued. "It's ugly and it's awful, and I've *got* to do something about it! I'm too embarrassed to be this way anymore." I sobbed uncontrollably into my soggy pillow as I collapsed on the couch in the den.

That was D-day for me, the day the diet began. My hatred of fat had escalated into a stark fury and this furious hatred of my fat translated into a furious hatred of myself.

That very moment I made a commitment that I was going to shed those ugly pounds regardless of the cost. I'll starve if I have to, I thought, but I am going to regain control over my eating and my body even if it kills me! I was determined to rid myself of that hideous flabby fat once and for all. I would never, ever allow myself to be fat again as long as I lived!

Having a good knowledge of nutritional requirements, I designed a sensible, healthy diet that included portions of food from all of the major categories: fruits and vegetables; grains and cereals; meats, fish, and poultry, and dairy products. I ate brunch, exercised moderately, drank an occasional glass of water, consumed a balanced dinner then waited thirty minutes before slowly sipping my dessert—an icy cold glass of milk.

Gradually the pounds began to dissolve and I regained a measure of self-confidence, emerging from my depression like a timid turtle slowly thrusting its head from the sanctuary of its protective shell.

By summer, remarks from friends, family, and even Warren were ego boosters instead of a rain of crushing blows. At 116 pounds I went to our family doctor for a general physical. He casually observed, "You seem to be the only one in your family who has a handle on their weight. Keep it up! You're doing fine!" Such innocent compliments fueled my fear-motivated discipline.

Slowly, subtly, almost imperceptibly, my meticulously healthful routine took on a new twist. In an attempt to spot-reduce the problem areas between my waist and my knees, I began to encircle them with Saran Wrap, which I tied on with pieces of yarn. With my legs covered like a couple of leftover drumsticks, my exercise would generate greater perspiration in the crucial locations. Normal liquid intake replenished the fluid loss but for a while I felt as if I was accomplishing something. Then, leafing through fashion magazines one day to covet the bodies of the models and measure my progress against them, I happened upon the ubiquitous back-page ads: "Melt away ugly fat in one hour!" "Lose inches with absolutely no effort!" "Watch those pounds disappear while *you* relax!"

I was just the customer they were trying to ensnare. After taking a tape measure to my hips and thighs, I sent in the requested information with the payment. I asked for two wonder-working gadgets and then waited for my mail-order miracles to arrive. The stretchy black leg wraps came in due time, but I had to write the company from which I had ordered my balloon pants to remind them that the arrival time had long since lapsed. When the blue, plastic "bermuda shorts" finally showed up, I followed the instructions by attaching the built-in nozzle on the right hip to our vacuum cleaner, tied the chords at the waist and knees, and watched my strange new garb inflate as the machine howled in my room. The hot air was supposed to melt away the fat. I must confess I was never impressed with the results.

My rubber leg bands, however, became my favorite body-altering gimmick. It seemed that there was always a noticeable difference in the girth of my thighs after putting them on for a few hours of exercise, or even wearing them as I slept. I praised them to my schoolmates, and one day after some intense persuasion on the part of a girlfriend, I loaned them to her. When she sheepishly informed me that she had broken them, it nearly cost our friendship! I had no way of replacing them so I had to find other ways to reduce.

The only alternative I could trust was to increase my exercise and decrease my caloric intake. Gradually I began skipping breakfast, assuring my parents that I would eat after my classes were finished. Once home from school I concocted blender beverages that looked rather substantial but consisted only of eight ounces of skimmed milk, saccharin, a tablespoon of instant coffee, and ice cubes. I nursed it along slowly, savoring every nutritionless spoonful. Sometimes I ate an apple or a salad with my own special dressing of vinegar, water, and artificial sweetener. Predinner eating could under no circumstances total more than 200 calories because the evening meal was the only one I was unable to escape. Although we sat together at the breakfast table for family devotions before school, I could avoid actually eating. Dinner, however, was the daily challenge. It was a family time and excuses for not partaking in this prepared meal were always rebuffed. Actually, by half-past six I was looking forward to some food.

In order to enjoy eating a decent dinner, I decided that my exercise would have to burn more calories. I began rising at six in the morning for coffee followed by a forty-five-minute jog in the alleyway behind our house. Back in my room I relaxed my tightened muscles with some yoga-type stretches and quickly dressed in my school uniform. Then I breathlessly joined the rest of the family for Scripture reading, hymn singing, and prayer, and drove my sisters to school. Still I was not satisfied. I exercised with the television experts, did aerobic dancing through the house to the latest top forty hits, and bought every booklet on diet and exercise the supermarkets, drugstores, and airport racks had to offer. But it was all too unorganized, too unstructured for my increasingly regimented approach to life.

Finally one Sunday afternoon as I was finishing up a term paper I had been putting off, I conceived of a way to wrap up the school project without becoming exasperated with the subject matter by interjecting exercises. For every twenty minutes I spent on my homework, I broke for ten minutes of calisthenics with each exercise session focusing on a specific feature of my body. That day I designed the blueprint for a daily program that I followed uncompromisingly to the most minute detail for years thereafter. Although I occasionally added new exercises for reducing the inner thigh or toning up the buttocks, I never subtracted a single leg lift or sit-up.

The plan I evolved for my cumulative daily ritual was a quick-paced, nonstop two-hour workout. I added swimming to the program and created a thirty-minute line up of activities starting with a set of spring bounces on the diving board followed by a specific number of laps swum with every type of stroke. I concluded the strenuous sequence with an array of exhausting water-kick leg exercises.

I recall one afternoon at the outset of my board bouncing when my mother strolled up to the edge of the pool and wistfully commented, "Boy, Cherry, you sure have gotten your legs in great shape!" I knew she was right and I wasn't about to let up now—not on your life!

Needless to say, the pounds continued to drop and at an even more accelerated rate. The exhilaration of controlling my body was propelling me further into frenzied levels of physical activity. My calorie-burning efforts were succeeding and allowing me to indulge in some of my unusual food fetishes. After a dinner of broiled chicken, I collected the bones and remaining skin from the other plates to supplement my own meal. That greasy, flavorful skin and the marrow inside the bones were two of my favorite delicacies. However, nothing could beat the brown, slightly shriveled, border of fat on the perimeter of a steak or, more heavenly yet, a juicy lamb chop. I became a scavenger whenever lamb chops were served, guarding against the return of any plate to the kitchen before I had the opportunity to descend on its remains like a vulture.

At this point in my life my entire existence seemed to revolve around my mandatory four hours of exercise while most of my thoughts gravitated towards menus, recipes, and caloric computations. What was left of my resources was reserved for schoolwork and performing. Leisure time was usually spent copying recipe ideas from magazines and newspapers. I still got straight A's and even while traveling weeks at a time I maintained my rigorous schedule of jogging, stretching, calisthenics, and swimming.

I was never without a specific dietary plan, whether based on daily caloric intake or the latest reducing fad. I was alternately committed to high protein and low carbohydrates, sold on high roughage and low protein, convinced of the high-fat and low-carbohydrate approach. I eventually incorporated an assortment of carefully balanced nutritional combinations and virtually any scheme that promised weight control as its guaranteed reward.

Rigid regimentation had taken over my life. Any disturbance of my painstakingly structured personal agenda was like yanking on a tightly held security blanket. I regarded phone calls from my closest friends as unforgivable interruptions.

That jerk! How dare she call me now? I would think to myself as I went to pick up the receiver. Intentionally, I would keep such conversations as brief as possible, having strategized my schedule to the very minute with no contingency plan for setbacks. Missing as little as a quarter of an hour of my compulsory calisthenics slammed me into an emotional tailspin—I could actually feel the difference the next day.

Likewise, any mealtime foul-ups or spur-of-the-moment changes regarding dinner practically heralded the end of the world for me. More than once an unassuming waitress was the target of my ravings over toast buttered when ordered dry or an entree swimming in sauce specified to come on the side. I was always the last one to order in a restaurant, the many options compounding my general inability to make decisions. My detailed questions and special requests for certain preparation methods would send the waiter back and forth until I chose something with which the kitchen could comply.

Although my obsessions began to make me a recluse, I somehow maintained minimal levels of social interaction. Relationships with my two or three best girlfriends and with Warren were the few that remained and even they were shadowed by clouds of impending doom. Only an occasional evening or small portions of the weekend were available for socializing, and those rare opportunities were limited to the months of the year when we were not performing.

Understandably for a seventeen-year-old girl in love, time spent with Warren was my highest priority. We were becoming increasingly serious about each other and were beginning to discuss the possibility of marriage—a prospect both exhilarating and frightening to me.

Talk of marriage usually leads to the subject of children. Warren, predictably, was expecting to have a large family because of his own family experience and the teachings of his faith. When I discreetly informed him one evening that my menstrual cycle had ceased, his deep concern was apparent.

My parents were also worried about this recent development, especially because I had been regular as clockwork since my eleventh birthday. While I found it slightly disconcerting, I assumed it was merely a temporary complication. I welcomed the respite from my monthly onslaught of painful cramps and uncomfortable fluid retention. However, it was eventually decided that a medical checkup was in order. My first visit to a gynecologist was arranged despite my deep fear of this inevitable encounter.

Dr. McDaniel became one in a long line of physicians and specialists who treated me for a variety of ailments. Since my eighth-grade efforts to avoid school, I kept the medical professionals in business. Although I hated needles, blood tests were becoming routine with my frequent trips to doctors' offices. A battery of tests was required for each new episode. The presence of unusual symptoms was undeniable but the findings were always inconclusive or totally inconsequential. For example, after my indiscriminate consumption of drugs prescribed for my parents, my physical symptoms resembled those of mononucleosis, but my blood count indicated the opposite of the expected red-to-white-cell ratio. Instead of too many red cells, I had too many white cells. Only I knew that they had been marshaled to combat the flow of foreign chemicals into my bloodstream.

Another stunt I performed that same year was self-induced fainting using hyperventilation. It was definitely one of my more effective ploys; however, I had not bargained on falling against my mother's hope chest on my way down. That incident necessitated a series of head X-rays to detect possible skull fractures. Later, when I repeated the tactic in the school bathroom, I fell straight back onto the hardwood floor with a crack! When I regained consciousness I was peering into the faces of several startled classmates in a state of glassy-eyed bewilderment. After this second fainting spell a broader range of tests was ordered, including an EEG, an EKG, chest X-rays, and an array of other diagnostic procedures. Of course they found nothing out of the ordinary.

One strategy designed to aid in the production of a school paper backfired in a way I had not anticipated. When diet pills were no longer available I decided to substitute No-Doz. I would take a tablet or two to crank up my sluggish metabolism, increasing the dosage for specific challenges. On this particular occasion, with a major project due the next day, I realized I would have to labor through the entire night to finish it. I had accomplished such tasks before with the help of a diet pill or two, so why not do it with the No-Doz . . . just this once? From my own experience I knew that the Eskatrol was much stronger than my over-the-counter counterpart so I swallowed the remaining thirteen tablets. I don't really like these pills anyway, I thought, so I'll just get rid of them.

When everyone had said goodnight, I crept to my bathroom, switched on the light, and began to work the graveyard shift. In the beginning I felt fine and was making headway on my assignment. After a while though, I started feeling strange—nauseous, tremulous, and, oddly enough, drowsy. My efforts became worthless so I decided to go to bed. I would just have to deal with the classroom consequences later.

As I started to rise from my sprawled position on the floor, dizziness overwhelmed me. Carefully I sat on the edge of the bathtub, bracing myself by holding onto the sink. Suddenly I began hallucinating, the room started to shrink away from me. I felt like Alice in Wonderland, rapidly growing into a giant after following the instruction "Eat me!" Everything looked so small and so far below me. My fear at seeing things change drastically before my eyes set my heart pounding at such a rate that I had to lie down. All I could think about was getting back to my bed and going to sleep. I crawled like a boot-camp recruit on an obstacle course until with slow, deliberate motions I hoisted myself up onto my bed and shakily pulled the covers up to my shoulders.

I began to use, one by one, all my tried and true methods for getting to sleep. Many nights I had found it difficult to calm down the whirlwind of thoughts and details stirred up by the day's events. I counted forward, backwards, odds, evens, in English, French, and German, until I would finally drift off in a sea of numbers. This time nothing was working. In fact, the longer I lay there the harder my heart beat until my chest was constricted with a burning, tight feeling. I tried to relax totally because I knew that fear would stimulate the flow of more adrenaline, which would accelerate my heart even more. I concentrated on taking long, slow, deep breaths while keeping perfectly still. I dared not exert myself. My singular focus at that moment was simply to breathe. I realized I was becoming so weak and dehydrated that I could no longer lift my arm off the bed. I couldn't even make a sound when I tried to call for help. All I could do was concentrate on inhaling and exhaling, and even that was becoming a major effort.

Finally, after several fearful hours of labored breathing, I began to see the first few hopeful rays of dawn's light slipping through the wooden shutters that stretched across my bedroom windows.

Thank God! I thought. I made it through the night! Now if I can just hang on until someone comes to get me for school, maybe I'll get help before it's too late. Still fighting against any flow of adrenaline that might increase the rate of my palpitations, I attempted to control my thoughts as I waited to be rescued from what I felt was my certain demise. At long last there was a tentative knock at my door.

"Cherry, can I come in? It's time to leave," Laury's voice preceded her. She slowly opened the door and, seeing the room still dark, the shades pulled and me in bed, she asked, "What are you doing, Cherry? School starts in fifteen minutes!"

I tried to answer, I even tried to lift my arm to beckon her to my bedside, but I had absolutely no strength left in me. My heart was practically pounding through my chest. Incredulous at my lack of response, Laury approached the bed. With every ounce of energy I could muster I urgently whispered with a parched mouth, "Go get Mommy! I'm having a heart attack!"

"Oh, come on, Cherry! You're not having a . . ."

"Go get Mommy! I think I'm dying!" My tone must have convinced her I was serious because she sprinted from the room and within seconds my mom was sitting at my side.

She questioned me about my symptoms and I told her everything—about my homework, the NoDoz, my hallucinations, and my nightlong battle to breathe. It was as if I was making a final confession before slipping over the edge. Once again I was carted off to the doctor's office to be checked and to my amazement was informed that I would have to have taken twice as many NoDoz to have done any real or permanent damage.

"The heart is a powerful muscle and it can take a lot more than most of us realize. You gave yours a real workout last night and I don't suggest you try it again. But you look as if you learned your lesson." The doctor dismissed me with instructions to rest and sip liquids until I regained my strength.

I followed his advice and by the end of the day I was

almost back to normal. The experience had caused me to examine my priorities. I honestly thought I was going to die so I had tried to put my life in order before facing ultimate judgment. I determined to give up my obsessions about school, diet, exercise, and other circles of self-centered activity. I had already caused Lindy and Debby to withdraw from me through my neurotic behaviors and hermit-like existence in my room. Definite barriers had long since been erected between us. Perhaps after my confrontation with the specter of death, I thought, I would be able to tear down those barriers. Unfortunately, the NoDoz incident did just the opposite. Laury, who had looked up to me with respect and admiration regardless of my increasingly odd habits, received this latest situation as a personal affront. If I loved her, why would I risk killing myself? Didn't I care enough for her, if not for myself, to stay alive?

And so, with a thoughtless attempt to complete a routine school project, I alienated my only remaining ally. I was all alone.

CHAPTER FIVE

The Starveling

Loneliness, real or imagined, is an insidious, draining brand of depression that is no respecter of persons. An active life, a busy schedule, and a social circle teeming with friends, family, and associates are not necessarily effective against this emotional and psychological cancer. In fact, the incongruence of the external flurry and the internal famine often feeds the disease. Such was the case with me, compounded by the realization that the culpability for my condition rested solely and squarely on my shoulders.

My self-imposed exile allowed me the freedom to sink deeper into a maze of increasingly neurotic behavior. Somehow, somewhere, my mind had taken a detour and my sensible attempts at discipline and control had undergone a conversion to self-destruction. Suddenly, I was motivated by a stark underlying fear that fueled my growing desperation and provided the impetus for the bizarre activities that were becoming more and more a regular part of my daily life.

Incredibly, in spite of my all-consuming obsession, I managed to maintain a flawless facade for the general public. My family knew better, but to outsiders I appeared to be the girl who had everything—good-looking, talented, and intelligent with a happy family, travel opportunities, a life in the limelight, celebrated friends, material comforts, the best of schools, spiritual fulfillment. What more could one ask for? I obviously had my life together, others might have thought. The front I had created was so effective at times that I had the ability to intimidate many of the adults who knew me casually. My outer shell exuded an intense but illusory self-confidence, and I guarded it carefully, if unconsciously. It must never crack; it had to remain impervious to the influences and pressures around me, and it had to conceal the inner turmoil with which I had become so intimately acquainted. By hiding it, by ignoring it, by paralyzing my emotions with my external preoccupations, maybe, just maybe, the pain might go away.

My secret struggles were so private that I was even able to veil them from Warren. Although he expressed concern regarding my continued weight loss, he never fully knew the extent to which my odd pursuits had taken me. Besides, I saw my problems as being more the result of family battles over my behavior than of the behavior itself. So the image I projected in what was supposed to be my most open and honest relationship was a false one. He sincerely cared for me and I did not want to jeopardize the solace I found in his adoration. Within a few months, however, that is exactly what I did.

The question of religious differences that we had attempted to gloss over earlier was now looming before us like a wall erected with the heavy stones of family tradition from generations past. A modern-day version of Romeo and Juliet, we tried to overcome the barriers that confronted us, and for two years I buried myself in study of his faith. With an open mind I pored over material both supporting and refuting its doctrine. Even with the blinding bias of young love, my final conclusion was that I could not in good conscience become a member of his church. Through a series of circumstances that seemed more than coincidental, I had to ultimately admit that all of the arrows pointed to a rejection of Warren's deepest beliefs, which meant putting an end to the relationship. Without spiritual unity in such a vital area of our lives, we knew we had reached a dead end.

I sat in my room tensely waiting for Warren to arrive at our house to hear the final verdict. It was a cool November evening but I was oblivious to the pleasant autumn atmosphere, totally consumed with a feeling of dutiful resignation. I knew what I had to do. There was no sense in postponing it any longer; it would only prolong the pain. Oddly, I almost felt relieved to have a definite direction to pursue after living in limbo for so long, and I felt that my loyalty must first be to God and my understanding of Him. It was not going to be easy but deep down I knew I was making the right choice and I believed that God would honor my sacrifice by bringing me an even better relationship, or fulfilling me in single life. After all, when Abraham raised the knife to offer up his only son, Isaac, hadn't the Lord, seeing Abraham's willingness to obey, provided a ram to sacrifice instead?

The doorbell rang. Suddenly my composure gave way to a shot of adrenaline I could taste on my tongue and feel surging through my chest. The time had come.

I met Warren downstairs in the family room, the long shadows of sunset accentuating the meaning of the moment. My parents and sisters had retreated to the second floor, leaving us alone in the dim light of dusk to at last resolve the cacophonic chord our lives had played together for months. One of us would have to change to create harmony, or the chord must be released. I knew Warren would not change, and I had finally decided that I would not convert for the sake of harmony with Warren at the expense of my own convictions. Softly, slowly I began to release that chord.

"Warren, I've done everything you've asked me to do. I've read, I've prayed, I've fasted, I've talked with missionaries, I've visited the temple, I've gone to your church, I've even met and spoken with your prophet. But I just can't agree with all that you believe, and I can't pretend to believe it myself. After my six days of fasting, at your request, I received an anonymous tape on the subject of your religion. I listened to it, not knowing whether to expect validation or criticism, but I listened to the whole thing. When it was over, Warren, I knew I had received my answer. I know you love the Lord, and you know that I do, too. Our first commitment is to Him, and He'll bless us for keeping that commitment. I just know it. But if neither of us is going to change, it doesn't make too much sense to pursue our relationship any further. I love you, and I've never known anything but wonderful experiences with you. But we've gone as far as we can go together and now it's time to part ways. I'll never regret anything in our relationship. I'll always remember it as one of the best parts of my life. There will never be another one like ours, and I've already decided that I will never settle for less than what we've had—even if that means having none."

To my shock, Warren seemed to crumble before my eyes. I had known he would not take it well, but I had no idea of the impact it would actually have on him. Immediately, I felt the strength with which I had broken my news begin to fade, like Samson having his superhuman power taken from him by one he loved. Within moments, the two of us were clutched in an emotional embrace with our sobs echoing through the house, the only sounds in the still night air.

Together we mourned our loss and when he finally left, drained and dejected, I returned to my room to wallow in my grief and to dwell on the self-loathing I felt for having hurt someone so dear.

Now more than ever before I plunged myself into a flurry of activity. From the moment I got out of bed in the morning until I retired at night, I was a perpetual-motion machine. The busier I stayed and the more I concentrated on caloric combinations, the less I had to think about the real issues in my life. Like a race horse wearing blinders I forged ahead free from distraction, with a singleminded focus on my goal and driven by the unseen burden I carried on my back. I buried myself in exercise, schoolwork, and food obsessions, coming out of my room only to jog, swim, eat dinner, or attend classes.

By my senior year of high school I had completed most of the required courses and had to spend less than three hours in the classroom each morning. Being an honor student, I was eligible for a program at U.C.L.A. enabling high-school seniors to begin some of their college credits early. I was grateful for the privilege and the recognition, but I was ambivalent about any additions to my meticulously scheduled routine.

Unable to allow myself to forgo such a prestigious opportunity, I arrived at a compromise. I decided to take one course, music theory, to keep my foot in the door with the U.C.L.A. honors program. Ironically, a class I assumed would come easily to me turned out to be a real challenge and I ended up loathing the entire experience. I had enjoyed songwriting and had written several songs that were impressive. I hoped my music class would augment my writing expertise but it frustrated me to analyze and dissect the only area left in my life that was creative and spontaneous.

Besides, my mind was too engrossed in counting leg circles and carbohydrates to be concerned with classics and quarter notes. With the help of one of the Boone show's backup musicians, I managed to pass the course, having learned little more than how to burn off more calories by riding my bike to and from class, or by walking briskly across campus and running up the steep stairway that left me breathless as the bell signaled the beginning of my daily hour of boredom.

In an attempt to help fill the emotional void left by Warren, my mother had taken me to pick out a pedigreed collie puppy that I promptly dubbed Summa (Latin for "greatest," "best," or "highest"). Even my pet had to be perfect. I don't know if the name was a projection of my own desires for personal attainment or if I simply expected of my puppy what I expected of myself. Whatever the reason, Summa became the object of my full emotional attention for the months that followed. Every day I cooked her breakfast with utmost care on our kitchen stove, making sure that all of her nutritional needs were met, and each night I put her to bed in the pool house with a heater and a night light. On a few occasions I slept out there with her. Of course, our daily walks were a must for her—and an extra hour of exercise for me.

Following my schedule from dawn to dusk would have made an Olympic trainer feel right at home. It read as follows:

6:00 A.M.—Rise, coffee, read Bible, dress for jogging.
6:30 A.M.—Jog four miles.
7:15 A.M.—Stretching exercises.
7:45 A.M.—Dress for school, join family devotions.
8:00 A.M.—Leave for school.

8:15 A.M.—English class at Westlake.

9:30 A.M.—Return home to feed Summa, prepare and eat coffee-and-milk drink, change clothes.

10:30 A.M.—Drive to friend's house.

10:45 A.M.—Ride bike or walk briskly to class at U.C.L.A.

11:00 A.M.—Music theory class.

Noon—Ride or walk to car.

12:15 P.M.—Drive home.

12:30 P.M.—Open time (homework, walk downtown, run errands, perhaps have small tossed salad with special low-calorie dressing).

2:00 P.M.—Walk Summa for one hour (maybe read and have apple during walk).

3:00 P.M.—Calisthenics in bedroom for two hours (some weight lifting).

5:00 P.M.—Prepare to swim, turn on sauna.

5:15 P.M.—Board bounces, lap swimming, leg exercises for forty-five minutes.

6:00 P.M.—Sauna.

6:15 P.M.—Shower, prepare for dinner.

6:30 P.M.—Dinnertime.

8:00–11:00 P.M. (or later)—Homework and prepare for bed.

The only feature of this Spartan schedule that an aspiring world-class athlete might find out of the ordinary would be the conspicuous absence of the all-important "training table." My energetic workouts were fueled by a single average meal. It was a well-deserved reward, my own gold medal for a job well done. Anything less than a perfect performance was inexcusable. Depending on the success or failure of achieving my daily goals, dinner became either the "thrill of victory" or the "agony of defeat."

One night at the end of a typical day of incessant activity, I wandered into my parents' bedroom. I came in to say goodnight but they were watching television so I sprawled on their bed to view the end of the program with them. I was wearing my regular nightly garb—sweatpants, a nightshirt, and socks. I chose this bedtime uniform partly because it was loose fitting (I hated wearing anything tight) and also because it seemed I was always cold. This outfit, with several layers of bed covers, kept me warm enough to sleep through the night.

I dozed off on my parents' bed, huddled on my side in a fetal-like pose. The next thing I knew I was aroused by the sound of my mother's crying, growing increasingly louder and more mournful despite Daddy's attempts to console her. She looked distraught, he looked anxious.

What happened, I wondered. Has the president been assassinated? The evening news droned on in the background. Has there been a death in the family?

"What's the matter? What's going on?" I asked urgently, only half-awake. My suddenly interrupted nap superimposed a dreamy, unreal aura over the scene before me.

While I lay sleeping, my mother had observed my fragile frame from across the bed. She noticed what appeared to be a pelvic bone projecting from my lower back, creating a sharp ridge under my sweatpants. For the first time in months perhaps, I was still enough and close enough to be observed carefully. My quiet sleep, so abnormal in comparison to my usual frenetic activity, undoubtedly prompted the scrutiny. She discerned several angular protrusions, contrasted by adjacent hollows and recesses. The overall

appearance was frighteningly reminiscent of the photographs of the survivors of Auschwitz.

Compelled by her curiosity, though fearful of what she
might discover, my mother reached across the bed and lifted
the end of my nightshirt enough to get a look at my back.
Horrified, she gasped and beckoned my dad.

"Pat, I can count every rib she's got! Her spine is actually
sticking out and her shoulder blades . . . Oh, Pat! She
looks like one of those Biafran refugees on the news!" She
began to cry, "What's wrong!? Is she sick? Is she dying?
She's wasting away right here in front of our eyes! What are
we going to do, Pat? Something's really wrong!"

Daddy was shaken by her sudden outburst and after
checking out my skeletal form for himself, he concurred.
He was encouraging Mommy to calm down and make an
appointment with the doctor the next morning when I
awakened.

"Cherry, honey, you're nothing but skin and bones!
We've got to take you in to see the doctor tomorrow and
find out what the problem is." My dad's voice continued as
did my mother's tears, but my attentiveness came to a
screeching halt as panic curbed my willingness to listen.

"I'm not sick!" I objected. "I feel fine! I don't need to
see a doctor!"

"Cherry," my mother moaned, "I just saw your back and
you look like a concentration-camp victim. You may feel all
right but you look like a skeleton!"

My anger was mounting as I realized that not only were
they threatening to jeopardize the area of my life that had
become most important to me, but they had invaded my
privacy! They had stepped beyond the firmly set boundaries
of my own personal modesty and looked under my shirt
while I was asleep! How could they!? I knew they had done

detective work before, hunting for diet pills or makeup. I knew they had listened in on a few phone conversations and monitored our rooms through our elaborate intercom system. I knew there had been an occasional phone call to verify our whereabouts. But there I was, seventeen years old, a senior in high school, going to U.C.L.A., almost old enough to vote or join the armed forces, and I had no authority over *my own body!* I was livid with rage!

"There is nothing wrong with me! I'm just thin! I don't feel sick and I don't need to see the doctor! And why were you looking under my clothes?!" I exploded.

My parents were taken off guard by my defensive response. They had no idea that their very natural desire to have me checked by a physician would be received as an outright attack.

"Cherry, I didn't have to look under your pajamas; I could see your bones *through* your clothes," my mom explained. "I was so shocked, I couldn't believe my eyes! I just lifted the back of your shirt to see if they were playing tricks on me. Honey, you may not feel sick, you may feel fine. But you're so emaciated. For *our* sake, for *our* peace of mind, we've got to have you checked! We wouldn't be responsible parents if we didn't do that much. We'll call Dr. Stark in the morning and set up an appointment. We just want to make sure there is nothing seriously wrong with you!"

"It's *my* body!" I argued. "I know how I feel, and I'm not sick! I'm not hurting anyone else by being thin, so why should it bother you? I'll tell you if I need a doctor. And why Dr. Stark? He's a pediatrician! Last time, I saw Dr. Newman, your doctor!"

"I know, honey, but you've only been to Dr. Newman once and Mommy thought you'd be more comfortable with

Dr. Stark. Besides, Dr. Newman can be a little salty sometimes," my dad's soothing, less emotional tone still carried the authoritarian sternness of a protective father.

"Well, if I have to see a doctor, I'll see Dr. Stark, but it's not fair!" I retorted. "I should never have come in to say goodnight!" With that, I stormed out of their room. Once in the sanctuary of my bedroom, I closed the door and turned on my closet light. I stared at myself in the full-length mirror mounted on the closet door. I removed my sweatpants, exposing my pale skin to the cold night air.

I don't look sick, I thought. I look fine! But they're going to make me go to the doctor and he's going to make me gain weight. I just *know* it! Why did I go in there tonight? Why didn't I just say goodnight and leave?! You idiot!

My self-deprecating thoughts multiplied within me as I feverishly exercised into the wee hours of the morning.

The next morning as I routinely made my way to the scale in my mother's bathroom closet, I was stopped by my father's voice coming from inside his own bathroom as I passed by on the way to my mechanical fortune teller. Darn, I thought. He's never in there when I come by! It was as if he had purposely perched there to pounce on me like a hungry bird of prey.

"I'll be there in a minute," I answered, hoping to read the magic numbers quickly and then respond to his call. But before I could begin my ritual weigh-in, Daddy emerged from his hiding place to ask me what I was doing.

"I was just going in to get some of that lemon face cream Mommy uses. My skin feels really dry." That story sounds believable and I came up with it in a split second! I felt proud and relieved.

"Well, since you're going in there anyway, why don't we just check and see how much you weigh so we can tell Dr.

Stark when we call him later." My dad's suggestion hit my panic button and I was at once filled with fear, anger, and resentment. I had to think fast.

"I usually weigh myself without my clothes so let me go in and step on the scale and I'll tell you what it says, okay?"

"Well, why don't you just leave them on this once and we'll just subtract a few ounces for your clothes," Daddy answered.

Caught! My mind raced madly in search of an escape.

"I usually go to the bathroom first and I have to go right now, so let me do that and then I'll weigh." That would give me a few minutes to guzzle some water at the sink, adding to the total.

"No, I don't think that'll make too much of a difference and it'll only take a second. Then you can go get dressed for school and . . ."

"But Daddy, I have to go to the bathroom!"

"I'm sure you can wait a few minutes, Cherry. Why are you fighting this? We just want to tell the doctor your weight. Now, come on. Let's see what you're down to these days."

As I stepped on the cold scale, the metal parts clanged and I acted surprised as I moved the small arrow down to zero. The large one rested in the notch that read 100 pounds. My dad reached over my shoulder and slid it to the 50-pound setting. I cringed as he pulled the little marker up to 50 and then tapped it farther and farther down, past 95 to 94, 93, 92.

"Ninety-two pounds, Cherry. Why? Did you know this already? Is that why you didn't want me to weigh you?" His questions seemed pleading and slightly pained.

I had no answers. Sheepishly I stepped down from the scale's platform—the miniature stage on which I had performed so admirably. It was now being reset for a new drama, with the same cast but with strangers vying for the role of director. This would be the scene of a battle of wills unparalleled in any previous production in the Boone family's Beverly Hills theater.

As I put on my school clothes, I cried tears of anger, fear, embarrassment, and confusion. I was angry that the incident occurred, afraid of what the consequences might be, humiliated at being forcibly weighed by my father, and confused about all the rest of my feelings. I felt naked, as though I'd been stripped, even raped. My power had been taken from me against my will, my secrets were no longer my own. How could they? How dare they? I was completely and utterly mortified.

They can't do this to me, I thought. I won't let them! I determined that no matter what the doctor said I was not going to give up—certainly not without a monumental struggle. My commitment reinforced, I set my jaw, clenched my teeth, and left for school prepared for war.

When I returned from my classes that afternoon, I was informed by my mom that the appointment with Dr. Stark had been made.

"He wants to see you at three o'clock, Cherry. Today."

I was unprepared for such a sudden confrontation. What would I say? Why today? And at three! That was precisely when I usually began my two-hour calisthenic workout! Why didn't they coordinate the timing with me first? I would have set it for one o'clock and skipped my salad, or even two and passed up my walk with Summa.

"What about my walk with Summa?" I asked, knowing that would elicit a more favorable response than an objection based on missing my exercise routine. It was ironic that they had chosen that particular time. It seemed as though they were already plotting against me in some kind of a calculated conspiracy.

"I'm sure she'll be okay if she misses one day. Besides, you can walk her when we get back if you want. I can't imagine we'd be back any later than five," my mother said.

"We'd better not. That's when I . . ." I caught myself before blurting out the rest of my thought.

"That's when you what, Cherry?" Mommy asked, detecting my reticence to complete the sentence.

"Swim," I mumbled, almost inaudibly, hoping she wouldn't hear me.

"Honey, Dr. Stark may have something to say about all this exercise. He may want you to slow down for a while, or even stop altogether if it's something, well, serious. We'll just have to wait and see what . . ."

"No! No! I won't stop exercising!" My emotions rose up inside of me like an erupting volcano. They can't make me stop! It's my body. I'm not doing anything to them! Why can't they just leave me alone? Before exploding, I raced up to my room, slammed the door, and cried. I felt like a caged animal, or an innocent victim of circumstances wrongly sentenced to the ultimate punishment. Trapped, helpless, no way out.

I had no one to whom I could appeal for pardon. Unless perhaps if the doctor found nothing wrong with me, he would let me off the hook! He might just pronounce a verdict of good health like Dr. Newman did last fall. He'd even encouraged me! It seemed like a long shot but it was my only remaining hope. Then realizing it was only 12:45, I began my calisthenics. I would finish just in time to leave at 2:45.

At 3:10 my mom's Cadillac rolled into the parking lot of Dr. Stark's Wilshire Boulevard office. We exchanged words during the ride from home over my tardiness. I had thrown in some extra knee bends and ran ten minutes late. Motivation for being punctual was obviously lacking.

The nurse ushered us into one of the private cubicles. I knew them all intimately from my numerous visits—plaques, certificates, artwork, equipment arranged slightly differently from room to room. I sat on the examination table, nervously kicking my feet back and forth as they dangled towards the linoleum floor. My mother sat in the chair across from me. Neither of us spoke. The only sound breaking the tension-filled silence was the swishing of my legs, the crinkling of the paper table covering beneath me, and the occasional squalling of a newly innoculated infant or the ringing of the phone. The smell of alcohol added subtly to the mounting fear.

Finally, the door opened and in walked the executioner. Maybe not, I encouraged myself, maybe not. Just wait and see.

"Hello, Cherry. Hi, Shirley. Well, what seems to be the problem here, young lady?" Dr. Stark asked, with his usual gentleness, and this time with puzzlement, too.

My mother answered, "She's been losing an awful lot of weight, Doctor, but we didn't realize how much until last night when I saw her bones coming through her clothes. She says she feels fine. In fact, she's more active than the rest of us put together. Pat exercises regularly but Cherry's even outdoing him. We were so concerned when we realized how thin she's gotten that Pat weighed her this morning. Dr. Stark, she's down to ninety-two pounds and she's five feet seven! That's when we decided to call you. There must be something wrong and we want to find out what it is and do something about it! She just can't keep losing like this!"

"How do you feel about this, Cherry?" he asked.

"I feel fine," I answered. I was too afraid to say more.

"Well, I know you weighed this morning, but let's step on the scale here and see what ours says," Dr. Stark suggested.

Good! He's not making me take off my clothes! That's bound to add up, I thought. I obediently, if reluctantly, slipped down from the table and walked to the scale. I was shocked when I saw the needle pointing to exactly ninety-two pounds. I had forgotten about the exercises and the missed meal. I had actually lost a pound or two since the morning weigh-in at home!

"Have you had any other strange symptoms, anything unusual or out of the ordinary? Dizziness, fainting spells, chilling, weakness, stomach pains, loss of menstruation?"

"Yes, doctor! She's complained of all of those things at one time or another, and she hasn't had a period in a year!" my mom replied, surprised at the coincidence.

"How about constipation, Cherry?" he directed his question at me as he poked at my lower abdomen. I knew he could feel the tightness, so I answered with guarded honesty.

"Yeah, I get constipated sometimes, especially when we travel." I tried to minimize the problem.

"How about your hair, your teeth?" he continued.

"That's right, Cherry! What was it Dr. Briskin said about your teeth last time you had them cleaned?" Mommy asked, searching her memory.

"My teeth are fine. I've never even had a cavity!" I responded defensively.

"I know, but he said something about your enamel coming off—eroding! That's it! He said her mouth looked like that of a middle-aged business executive with ulcers!" she added, giving the full report. I cringed with each word she spoke. Every time she opened her mouth it was like driving one more nail into my coffin.

"Your hair looks pretty brittle and dry, Cherry. Is that a new development?" Dr. Stark observed as he carried on with his examination.

"Just the ends. I swim a lot and the chlorine dries it out. Also, I have to blow it dry afterwards so I've been getting some split ends lately. Why?" I asked, fearful of his answer.

"Well, I've seen this kind of thing before and you seem to have all the same symptoms as the other cases I've heard about. And that's one of them. Shirley, Cherry, why don't you go into my office and I'll be in in a minute," he assured us as he left the room.

My heart was pounding, my hands were cold and clammy, and my thoughts raced as we waited one more time for the doctor to join us. Mommy commented on the uncanny presence of the various symptoms he had asked about. I sat silently.

"There's nothing really wrong with you physically that I can see, Cherry," Dr. Stark announced as he sat down at his desk.

I knew it! Just tell them to leave me alone, I thought.

"But you are severely underweight. And since I can't find an indication that it's due to illness of any kind, I have to believe that you're the only one who can do anything about it. Now you can cooperate and put on some weight by yourself, or I'm going to have to reserve you a bed at Children's Hospital where we can do it for you."

The words struck me like bullets from a firing squad. I was in shock. Slowly, as I realized the impact of what he had said, the tears began to fill my eyes.

"Now, do you think you can do that?" Dr. Stark's tone was kind, but firm.

"I don't know," I whimpered. "I guess so. But how much weight?" My fear was obvious.

"I'm not going to quibble with numbers right now, dear. If I had to be pinned down I'd say you need at least twenty pounds, but the main thing is you just have to stop losing and start putting some back on before you endanger your life."

I peered through blurred, watery eyes at his concerned, bespectacled face. His tan complexion, his dark hair sprinkled with gray, his white shirt fastened at the neck with a black tie—everything faded from my consciousness as I envisioned all of my blood, sweat, and tears, all my dieting, all that hard work suddenly becoming worthless. Had it all been in vain? I pictured that fat, flabby, frustrated, 140-pound girl I had come to detest so deeply one year before. The mere thought of her filled me with terror. She haunted me daily, always in the back of my mind, always sharing the mirror with me when I viewed my reflection. No matter how hard I tried to escape, she was omnipresent, threatening to take control. Now I was being forced into unconditional surrender.

"Can I still exercise?" I asked, swallowing the lump in my throat.

"Cherry, I'm not going to tell you what you can and can't do. I suppose some moderate exercise would be all right. But remember, you must compensate for that by eating enough to gain weight or I'll have to put you in the hospital. I mean it!"

With that, Dr. Stark led us out of his office. As Mommy and I drove home through thick rush-hour traffic, my mind replayed the horrible nightmare I had just endured. The options before me were equally abhorrent. I could slow down my exercise, eat more food, and gradually inflate into the monster I was so desperately fleeing, or I could continue my weight control efforts and ultimately end up in the hospital—*Children's* Hospital at that! Almost eighteen years old and still considered a child! I could just see myself strapped to a bed with guard rails at either side, a needle buried in my arm, pumping me full of sugar round the clock, unable to do anything about my plight. In my imagination it became a torture chamber, further exaggerated by the images of young children laughing at an older person who was being constrained to undergo this unusual ordeal. I would have absolutely no control over *anything*. The thought terrified me! Somehow, I would have to come up with a plan to placate the ruling powers. My parents and the doctor would have to see me actually gain at least a few pounds soon or the reins of my life would certainly be torn from my grip.

My mom broke into this chain of thoughts in as pleasant and encouraging a tone as she could muster.

"Well, honey, would you like to stop at the grocery store on the way home and choose some things you'd like me to fix for you? How about some lamb chops tonight?"

"You don't have to fix anything for me. I can do it myself." I hadn't counted on yielding control over my menus and recipes.

"Well, why don't we just stop by and pick up some of your favorite foods so we'll at least have them available at the house," she suggested, fully intending to do so regardless of my apparent lack of enthusiasm.

As we perused the aisles of the Beverly Hills Food Giant, I fought the sights and smells that seemed to jump out at me from the shelves. The fact that I was going to *have* to eat more than usual and exercise less was inescapable. With these forced conditions my solid-steel willpower began to melt ever so slightly. The issue was not "will I eat?" It was rather "what will I eat?" This was opening up an area I had kept shackled in my subconscious. Abruptly all of my food fantasies were coming to the surface and in spite of attempts to ignore them, my stomach and my deprived taste buds screamed to be satisfied. Surprisingly the thought of eating whatever I wanted without driving myself to exercise five hours a day appealed to me. I felt a momentary sensation resembling relief.

I put granola cereal, peanut butter, half-and-half in the shopping cart, salivating at the thought of a lucious combination of all three. I noticed my mom adding prunes, ice cream, and a large assortment of cookies.

Quickly I objected. "Hey, I don't want to eat a bunch of junk food!"

"You don't have to eat this stuff if you don't want to. There are other people in the house who will. Besides, you may change your mind. These things would help you put on some weight in a hurry and Dr. Stark seems to be interested in some quick results."

Reality burst upon me like a torrential flood. My control was already awash. I had to get home. Maybe I could still swim before dinner. As I replaced the food fantasies with frantic mental scheduling, basal metabolic rate estimates, and total caloric intake, I focused on a goal of one pound a week weight gain. That felt safe and would undoubtedly quiet the worries mounting in the minds of my parents and doctor.

That night, dinner was chicken with vegetables, rice, and salad. I had eaten that meal many times with no problem. Mommy, however, had voiced her plans to create a special milkshake for me later in the evening and I had no idea what its contents would be. To ensure against surpassing my predetermined daily allowance I decided to avoid eating dinner. I came up with the perfect scheme.

The dinner gong sounded. As we filled our plates at the stove I informed Mommy that I was going to take my food to my room so I could study while I ate; after all, the trip to Dr. Stark's office interrupted my homework. She agreed; I knew she didn't want to rock the boat at that moment. My parents complied with nearly every request I made at that point—anything to make me happy and heavier.

I smuggled a plastic bag upstairs with me. When I was sure they were all preoccupied, I spooned my food into the bag, sealed it up, and hid it in one of my dresser drawers. I couldn't put it in the trash—my mother might see it. I couldn't flush it down the toilet—the drumstick wouldn't fit. Besides, the thought of wasting it was unthinkable. Later on I would pull the meat from the bone and put it in Summa's dish with the rest of my dinner. Then I would be able to have the milkshake free of guilt and my meal would not be wasted.

When a respectable amount of time had lapsed I rinsed my dish in the kitchen as if I had fully enjoyed supper. My mom was standing over the blender with a spoon in her hand and several items on the counter. My calculator-brain began clicking away: ice cream, prunes, peanut butter, half-and-half. I could only estimate the total. I never ate these foods and I wasn't familiar with their calorie content.

"What all are you putting in there?" I queried nervously.

"Oh, you'll like it! It's really good. Want a taste?" She extended a tablespoon.

"No thanks. I'll wait," I answered, racking my brain for the right numbers. This challenge was to be greater than I had anticipated.

Finally, Mommy entered my room with the finished

product in a tall soda glass complete with straw and long-handled teaspoon. It was as thick as mashed potatoes and the color of gravy—at a glance, very unappetizing. But I knew the ingredients would compensate for its appearance with an appealing taste. But so much!

"I'm still a little full from dinner, Mommy. Can you put some of it in a smaller glass and save the rest?"

"Just drink what you want and if it's too much you can put the rest away. You might like it enough that you'll want to finish the whole thing!"

That's what I was afraid of, I thought to myself. "Besides," she added, "you should probably stretch your stomach a bit so you can begin eating more." As she closed the door her last remark resonated ominously. Stretch my stomach! That's precisely what I *didn't* want to do.

Once again I had to come up with a solution. I went into the bathroom and poured half of the concoction into the toilet, flushing it quickly. Returning to my books I slowly sipped the rest, savoring every creamy, sweet ounce. It was so incredibly rich—the part of it I ate sat like lead inside me—yet my mouth thrilled to every spoonful. In fact, I drew out the pleasure as long as I could, spending several minutes on each teaspoon's dense load. The drink was too viscid to be drawn through the straw although it was a thoughtful and decorative touch. It was more fun to eat it from the spoon, anyway: to play with it, look at it, smooth the lumps with my tongue, divide each bite in thirds. No homework was done. I was lost in the wonders of that milkshake.

When it was gone I licked the spoon clean and, with my finger, gleaned the last few drops on the sides and bottom of the glass. Suddenly, I wished I hadn't disposed of the other half of it. My sense of taste had been titillated for the first time in months and it seemed to be waking up from a kind of hibernation, remembering and craving those wonderful things of which it had been so systematically deprived.

My chicken! It was still in the drawer—that's what I can finish off with, I thought, deciding that the salty flavor would counteract the syrupy sweet film that still coated my mouth.

Just as I reached into the drawer for my plastic bag, there was a knock on my door. Before I could scramble to replace it, my mom entered the room and I quickly shoved the drawer shut with my foot.

"What do you want?" I demanded, anxiously trying to hide the bag.

"What are you doing, Cherry? What have you got in your hand?"

"Oh, uh . . . I just, uh, gathered some scraps from dinner to take out to Summa. Why?" That sounded reasonable, I thought.

"I didn't see you in the kitchen," she observed suspiciously.

"Well, I got it earlier when you were busy making my drink. It was very good but I'm so full now. I feel stuffed." Perhaps I could distract her before she deduced the truth, I hoped. It didn't work.

"Why did you put it in a bag instead of in her dish, Cherry?" Her bewilderment at my behavior was obvious.

"Oh, I don't know. I guess I just forgot," I sputtered. That was real stupid, I accused myself silently.

Mommy came closer and saw the whole drumstick, untouched, through the plastic, amidst the lettuce leaves and confettilike peas and rice. The facts began to dawn on her as she confronted me.

"Cherry, that piece of chicken isn't a scrap! Now, where did this come from? Did you eat your dinner?"

"Yes, I ate my dinner. This is from the kitchen. I got it from the leftovers." I altered my story slightly.

"Since when do you give Summa whole pieces of chicken?" she challenged.

"I was going to scrape the meat off of the bone for her."

"This seems awfully suspicious, Cherry. Are you telling me the truth?"

"*Yes!* I'm telling you the truth. Don't you trust me? I drank the whole shake, too!" My lies compounded.

"How do I know you just didn't throw it all down the toilet?"

"I drank it! Honest, I did!" I sensed she was beginning to back down.

"Well, give me the bag. I'll put the chicken back and empty the rest of this into Summa's dish. I hope you're not lying to me, Cherry. I would be very happy if you did eat your whole dinner and drink that whole milkshake, but you have to admit, this all looks pretty unusual." She left the room with my dinner and closed the door.

Darn it! Why did she have to come in here right when I was getting that bag? She didn't even wait for me to tell her to come in. And now she's got my food and most likely she doesn't believe a word I said! What a stupid story.

My self-flagellation continued as I prepared for bed and sat down with my books. It was futile attempting to study. All I could think of was that chicken. I would have to be much more careful next time. I'll show her, I thought, with her fancy drinks and fattening foods. I'll just dump out the *whole* milkshake next time! And I'm going to eat that chicken—right now!

I slipped into the kitchen, careful not to disturb the rest of the family in the den watching television. To get to the refrigerator unnoticed I had to crawl across the floor behind the breakfast table and then pray that no one saw the light go on as I opened the door. It was like a daring commando raid.

Once I was sure that I was safe, I proceeded to search for what was rightfully mine. I moved a few items from one shelf to another in the crowded cooler in an attempt to claim my possession. I reached for the small foiled mound, uncovered my treasure, and took a bite. As I closed the door and turned around to slither back to the hallway with my prize, I saw Mommy standing in front of me. I recoiled with shock.

"What are you doing?" she asked.

My mouth was full of chicken. I frantically tried to come up with an explanation as I chewed and swallowed.

"I'm just eating some of that piece of chicken I was going to give Summa before," I replied, still startled by her presence.

"You said you were full from your dinner and milk-shake," she recounted with a hint of disbelief.

"Well, I just thought since I had messed it up in that bag with the leftovers nobody else would want it so I decided to come get it." That sounded innocent enough, even considerate.

"You could have had it for lunch tomorrow if you're so full tonight." She saw through my lie.

"Well, I guess I just wanted it now. That drink was so rich I needed something that wasn't sweet to get rid of that taste in my mouth."

"This whole thing is very strange, Cherry. But I'm not going to complain as long as you're eating. I just hope you're being honest with me."

"I am," I reassured her as I climbed the stairs. I

desperately wanted to get away from her. Why was she always there at the worst times? My frustration and anger began to boil over as I ate my chicken, first nibbling single strands of the striated meat, then sucking the marrow out of the bone, and finally stuffing the crunchy skin into my mouth. She's just glad I'm eating, I thought. Now I've eaten too much tonight, thanks to her. I've eaten far too much.

The realization overwhelmed me with fear. They were going to be forcing food on me continually and I would simply have to outsmart them. They couldn't make me eat anything I didn't want to. I wouldn't let them. I had to be in control of my weight gain or it just would not happen.

As I pondered my plight, my emotions intensified and the food in my stomach seemed to expand like a sponge, churning with the acids my anxiety was producing. What could I do? This was only the beginning of the process of putting on the pounds, and I was miserable.

It was then I recalled a way in which I could alleviate my discomfort. Throwing up. It seemed the only way out. I locked my bathroom door, leaned over the toilet, stuck my fingers down my throat, and heaved until nothing more would come up.

"Cherry, are you all right?" My mother's voice filtered through the wooden door. The door knob rattled as she tried to come in. "What's going on in there?"

"I, uh . . . I guess that drink was a little too rich for me, Mommy. I just threw up," I answered, sounding as sick as I could.

"Why is the door locked?" she asked.

"I don't know. I didn't realize I had locked it." I reached over and opened the door. As the stench wafted past her, she winced.

"Did you do this on purpose?"

"What do you mean?" I responded with a hurt expression on my face.

"You know what I mean. You made yourself throw up when you missed so much school that one year—you confessed that to us several times! Is that what you're doing now? Is that why you weigh ninety-two pounds?" She was becoming angry.

"No, I'm not! I haven't done that in years!" I raised my voice defensively. Not until tonight, I thought.

"Why is vomit all over your hand, Cherry? Are you telling me honestly you didn't force yourself to throw up?" She didn't believe me one bit. Strange as it now seems, I was deeply incensed that she did not trust me.

My mother finally left the room confused, suspicious, and afraid of what I was doing to myself. I was relieved that the day was over. My emotions had run the gamut, from compliance to defiance, from acceptance to resistance, from flexibility to rigidity, from peace and openness to outrage and fear. Feelings of instability and vulnerability were more unsettling than I could consciously acknowledge. Instead of squarely facing them I decided to push even harder for my perceived rights to exercise control over my own body. I went to sleep that night determined not to let anyone else have more than I was willing to give.

That day was a landmark in my life. It marked the beginning of four years of constant conflict with my parents over food and weight. Did I eat too little? Had I eaten too much? Did I keep it all down? Had I thrown it up? Had I gained any weight? Did I weigh enough? Did I exercise too much? Had I exercised at all? Was I being honest or was I telling lies?

During this time I graduated with honors from Westlake and became a freshman at U.C.L.A., maintaining an A average to assure my continued membership in the honors program. The shock of going from a senior high-school class of seventy girls to a sea of ten thousand freshmen was intimidating to say the least. I spent as little time there as possible. I enjoyed attending some of the athletic events; in fact, some of the star athletes were my friends and classmates. However, the largest portion of my energies was spent on pursuing physical perfection, as I perceived it, regardless of my parents' attempts to coerce me into conforming to their image of me—an image supposedly designed with my ultimate health and happiness in mind.

Daddy had set what seemed to me to be a rather arbitrary lower weight limit of 110 pounds. How could he know what was best for me or for my body? The pressure to reach that enchanted number was relentless and I resented it, stubbornly refusing to submit. When called to a mandatory supervised weigh-in, I used a number of techniques to manipulate the scale's report. I would drink as many as eight glasses of water before entering my mom's bathroom, hiding my misery until after the ritual, at which time the water was regurgitated into a toilet with the force of a fire hose. Once I even hid some two-pound dumbbell weights in the back pockets of my shorts. The effect was exactly what I had hoped for, until my mother lovingly patted me on the rear and uncovered my metal additions. After the four extra pounds were removed to reveal that I had actually lost instead of gained, I was reprimanded.

Punishments took various forms during these troubled years. They ranged from suspended privileges to spankings, which I received as late as eighteen years of age. Once I had run off to Warren's with a car and a permit, and was not allowed to get my license until six months after my sixteenth birthday. If I was caught lying, vomiting, taking overdoses of laxatives, or similar infractions, a special movie, a certain date, or an eagerly awaited event was canceled. At times, there were attempts at reasonable discussion, but usually it was a fruitless effort.

My parents were frustrated at seeing absolutely no change in my attitude or behavior after months of contention. My dad decided that if I was going to act like an obstinate child I should be treated like one. At five foot seven and 92 pounds, perhaps I even looked like one. He raised the 110 pound goal to 115 pounds since I had refused to accept his first more liberal offer. I could have killed myself for not making it to 110 pounds at least once to appease him. I was furious.

On at least two occasions I remember being turned over his knees and spanked—once at seventeen and once at eighteen. The first one came after being discovered throwing up and then denying it; the second one came after picking Lindy up at school and then deciding to go to see the Osmonds for a quick visit without asking or informing my parents. When we finally arrived home Mommy was distraught with worry. Ambulance sirens screaming through our intersection and reports of some major collisions over the radio had not helped calm her runaway imagination. Daddy was totally exasperated and before we could join the other girls at dinner, he proceeded to turn Lindy and then me over his knees.

The spanking was painful and very humiliating, but the worst of it was watching Lindy get punished, knowing all the while that she was an innocent passenger, guilty only by association. In a way this final spanking I received ultimately hurt Daddy as much as it did me because for the next two weeks he had to look at the marks on the backs of my legs. Even though his blows had been no harder than usual, the fact that I had no subcutaneous padding to soften the impact resulted in a steady visual reminder to him of his hasty reaction to our harmless outing, and he regretted it.

Moreover, I no longer welcomed punishment as a cathartic experience, as I had in earlier years. I had come to view it as something to avoid. I felt this kind of extreme response was unwarranted except perhaps in cases of my increasing deceptiveness. But I felt that my parents were forcing me to lie by not letting me pursue my own course of diet and exercise. Because they were demanding that I eat more and exert myself less, I began regularly gorging myself and vomiting, exercising in secret, swallowing entire boxes of laxatives, shoplifting, and, of course, lying about all of the above. I totally disregarded the potential consequences of my increasingly bizarre actions. For me, unless I was caught and subsequently punished, there were no consequences. At least that was how I viewed the situation.

I suppose it never occurred to me that being caught shoplifting could lead to real legal prosecution. Perhaps I had simply convinced myself that I would not be detected— I was very careful, always aware of alert store managers on patrol, scanning video cameras, and one-way mirrors. When I was on a binge, I took food—a box of cookies, a pack of Twinkies, a six-pack of candy bars. When I wanted to counteract a binge, I stole laxatives. In both cases, I couldn't justify paying money for what would most assuredly be flushed down the toilet in a matter of hours. Plus, it would have cost me a small fortune. So instead, I rationalized that theft was preferable to waste, and no one would miss the few items I cautiously slipped into a pocket or purse as I pretended to be hunting for other imaginary items on my nonexistent shopping list.

My physical sense of self had become so preeminent that my emotions, intelligence, and even my principles dropped significantly on my scale of priorities. I had to see what I *wanted* to see in the mirror or I could not feel good about myself. My body image determined my self-esteem. No fat, no flab equaled no fear, no failure. That false sense of security made it all seem worth it—the pain, the discomfort, the fatigue, the guilt.

Although I went into the battle with my parents convinced that I was doing no harm to anyone, including myself, I could not help beginning to feel a nagging sense of guilt—not for my desire to be skinny but for what I was doing to my family in my efforts to fulfill that desire. The endless chain of arguments, confrontations, and feuds always accompanied by raised voices, frustrations, and tears was wearing thin on us all. I knew I was hurting my parents by my lying, stealing, and other habits. I believed that by disobeying my parents I was also disobeying and displeasing God. The guilt was mounting with each misdeed and I was succumbing to increased feelings of self-hatred. Ultimately I reached a point where I knew I needed to amend my disruptive habits. Only by giving in, by giving up my obsessions with food and weight, by relinquishing the preoccupation with my body would there be peace of mind and peace at home.

I began sincere efforts to change my behavior: eating without vomiting, foregoing an occasional hour of exercise, having a substantial meal without allowing it to trigger a binge. In spite of my attempts, however, the other part of me (apparently the more influential part) always succeeded in undermining my good intentions. My neurosis had become too deep and too obsessive to be easily dismissed. Instead, I was in the grip of an emotional octopus, immobilized in a tangle of tentacles. My mind was in the coils of a huge psychological python, strengthening its suffocating squeeze with the slightest hint of a struggle for freedom. Incredibly, the area of my life in which I had prided myself for having total control had now taken control of me, so much so that I was feeling trapped and helpless. I was sinking in quicksand.

Unable to help myself, I consented to occasional outside counseling when it was suggested by my parents or by others. These sessions included several lengthy discussions, followed by even lengthier times of prayer, concluding with tears, commitment, and intense levels of resolve. Each session felt like a spiritual, emotional, and psychological breakthrough. One weekend trip to visit a pastor friend led to an entire evening of prayer for deliverance from my bondage. We continued until I exploded into uncontrollable rage, screaming at the top of my lungs until I was hoarse. Some may have called it an exorcism of sorts. I believe it was the first time I had ever permitted myself to vent anger stored up for years with no outlet for expression.

I remember praying and talking with the pastor of our church, Jack Hayford, more than once regarding my circumstances. He, too, felt that there was a buildup of tension, of unrelieved stress that was manifesting itself in my rigid and inflexible approach to life. He felt that I was being given two alternatives: life or death. It was up to me to make the critical choice. I told him and myself I wanted to choose life. My follow-up on that choice seemed to fall pitifully short. Somehow I could not actualize those choices and the changes they necessitated.

Another revealing time of discussion led to an important insight that seemed like a pivotal key in the unlocking of my chains. A couple who were close friends of my parents were discussing with me my perfectionism and my striving to achieve. They speculated that perhaps I was living in my father's shadow and trying desperately to measure up to his image, to match his reputation for multifaceted accomplishments at an early age. Assuring them that my parents were applying no pressure on me to be such a high achiever they responded that whether it was passed on to me verbally was not the issue but that my perception of their desires could create the same pressures.

As I considered their words I knew that my mom and dad never so much as hinted that they had been displeased with me as a child or that I wasn't living up to their expectations. However, among my earliest and even fondest memories were jokes about not being the son Daddy had wanted so badly. Both Mommy and he had planned for a boy. There was even a lengthy production number in his nightclub act that told the story of how we girls were born, disappointing him each time. "What a lovely sister she'll be to Mike!" he sang about me. "Got my four girls, want no more girls, all I need now is a boy!" were some of the lyrics in the final musical segment of his "soliloquy." At the time I loved every minute of it. He was, after all, singing about me. Suddenly, however, I saw that early input in a new light.

In spite of these halting but hopeful steps towards wellness there always seemed to follow a groaning collapse into captivity. Doctors, psychologists, pastors, evangelists, friends, and family all participated in throwing me a lifeline. Each time, regardless of how firmly I felt my hands grasping for rescue, it slipped through my fingers. I felt more and more despondent with each attempt.

My time must surely be running out, I thought, if not for my physical life, certainly for my spiritual one. My relationship with God was reduced to an occasional whimper for assistance immediately turning to guilty self-condemnation for my repeated stumbling or even for asking Him to help someone so unwilling to cooperate. I felt hopelessly unworthy. Even during traditional times of setting goals and making hopeful resolutions an atmosphere of desperation enveloped me like a thick fog.

On my nineteenth birthday I began a personal journal with this entry, the most positive attitude I could muster:

> July 7, 1973, Fairmont-Roosevelt Hotel, New Orleans, Louisiana. Well, today I am nineteen years old and for the first time in several years I actually woke up feeling older. Another reaction I had this morning was a feeling of remorse and shame that I haven't made better use of the past nineteen years. My remorse and shame were not for things I could have done or ways I could have impressed people but rather for the way I've stunted the growth of my relationships with other people, especially with the Lord.
>
> I could be so much further along in my spiritual development and emotional maturity if I could just keep myself out of the number-one position for any length of time. I hate my "roller-coaster relationships." I need consistency, stability, balance, self-control, and, most of all, joy.
>
> If I can just block out the patterns I've fallen into, learn from the mistakes. If I can just take one minute at a time, asking myself with each decision, "Is it right?" Maybe this year will make the last nineteen worthwhile.
>
> I want to rebuild trust, get myself in perspective, and become a person who can handle responsibility and honor my words.

Finally, after repeated failures I reached the limits of dejection. Following a major contest with my mother about my abstinence, overindulgence, subsequent self-purging, and obligatory denial in the face of hard evidence, I was overwhelmed with a feeling that I was plummeting downwards in a bottomless pit. Nothing and no one could stop me—not even myself.

That night I again crumpled to the floor in a heap crying out, "I want to die! I want to die! God please take me. I can't go on like this! Please end my life!" I pounded my head with my fists and continued beating myself and pleading to be put out of my misery until my face was swollen almost beyond recognition from the tears and screaming. I didn't have the courage to commit suicide and I knew that would be the ultimate infliction of pain on my parents and on God. But I was hurting so deeply I wanted it to stop at any cost, even if that meant ending my life. I hoped beyond hope that God would hear and answer at least this one prayer—a petition that was becoming a dolorous refrain.

Later that night my mother came into my room to have a quiet chat with me. Daddy was out of town and had missed the most recent contention over the same old issues. She sat down on the floor next to me.

"I'm sorry for the outburst today, honey, but I don't know what to do anymore. I'm stuck. I just don't know how to help you," Mommy confessed.

"I know. Me too. Sometimes I really want all of this to be over but I can't stop wanting to be thin." I waited a moment and then asked, "Mama, please don't tell Daddy I failed again. He doesn't have to know about it."

"Cherry, I've done that for you before and it only created more trouble. I can't do that. I have to tell him; my responsibility to him is to be honest with him and I'm not going to be put in the middle anymore. I won't make that mistake again, honey."

"But Mommy, *please*, just this time. I won't ask you to do it again, I promise! Please don't tell him!"

I began sobbing at the thought of yet another negative report to Daddy.

"Cherry, I have to! I may not know what else to do for you but I do know that keeping secrets from your father won't help you. I've pleaded your case to him before, I've believed you when he suspected you were lying. Now I can't cover for you anymore. Daddy has been right and I've been wrong and I can't betray his trust."

"But this will help, I promise! I'll try again! I'll try harder! I'll do *anything!* Just please, please don't tell him I've blown it again," I sobbed into my hands.

"If this is your idea of my only way to help you, then I give up. I can't do it! I give up, Cherry."

Suddenly I felt as if I was hanging from the edge of a cliff. "No! Mommy no! Please! No! You can't give up! Please! Don't leave me alone! Don't give up on me, Mommy, please!"

CHAPTER SIX

"A Jewelry-Draped Skeleton"

I buckled my seatbelt and closed my eyes as the jet engines whined and the 727 lumbered, then raced down the runway, accelerated, and lifted into the sky with the grace of a soaring bird. The city shrinking below us had been the scene of another showdown with my parents so I felt no desire to look back at it as we sailed through the clouds. Instead, all I wanted to do was put the entire ugly ordeal out of my mind: the dieting, exercise, weakening willpower, gorging, purging, hiding, confrontation, denial, shouting, tears, guilt, and desperation. The pattern was all too familiar now and I loathed every link in the chain. If I could just sleep and give my mind and my emotions a rest from their endless tribulations. And besides, if I'm asleep, I thought, the stewardess won't bother me with lunch. The last thing I need is another outburst like the previous evening!

The hiss of the jet was lulling me off into a welcome state of unconsciousness when I felt a tap on my shoulder. Go away, I thought drowsily, I don't want anything. Again, tap-tap and a voice calling my name, "Cherry. Cherry. Wake up, honey, I think you'll want to see this."

There was an excited urgency in my mother's voice. I

opened my eyes, squinting at the sudden influx of sunlight blazing through the unshaded window at my side. As my vision adjusted and focused on the object of Mommy's anxious attention, I saw an opened newsmagazine and my mom's finger hovered over an article.

"Read this, Cherry! Daddy saw it and passed it on for you to see. I think this is a real answer to prayer!" Mommy claimed hopefully as she handed me the magazine.

As I read the heading my heart literally skipped a beat— "The Self-Starvers." The words seemed to jump off the page.

Certain key phrases stood out as I scanned the one and a half columns of print: "frenzied level of physical exercise . . . fear of sexuality . . . menstruation almost invariably ceases . . . obsession with slimness and achievement . . . want to reassure themselves that they are really in control." The description given of a typical "self-starver" read like an autobiographical sketch: "mostly females in their early teens, intelligent, ambitious, middle- and upper-class girls who are perfectionists and eager to please their mothers and fathers" with "a terrible fear of not being good enough, of not doing what is expected of them." It continued to say that they "usually come from families that have conflicts but are 'enmeshed' in togetherness" and their behavior can be seen as a "symbolic 'oral rebellion' against overcontrolling and troubled parents."

I was not alone after all! There are others out there like me, going through the same turmoil, feeling insane and isolated. And this condition even had a name—anorexia nervosa. It has been occurring "more frequently in the past few years," the author reported, and it has "purely psychological origins." Doctors know about this thing, and people are being treated for it regularly! I may be crazy but at least I'm not the only one suffering under this curse, and maybe there is a cure! Maybe there is hope for me, maybe I can finally be well.

With great excitement I reread the contents of the eight short paragraphs, searching for any kind of prognosis for recovery. My discovery was sobering at best—"5 to 15 percent of known victims of anorexia nervosa have starved to death despite treatment." The final sentence restated the seriousness of the problem, calling it a "life-threatening disorder" that "may be more common than we ever thought."

After reading the article several times, my reaction was mixed. I was relieved to learn that I was not a freak, that there was a name for my condition, others who were victimized by it, and doctors who specialized in its treatment. However, I was also frightened, not so much by the prospect of death but that the disorder was psychological in nature and that it could require both psychotherapy and hospitalization. Neither of these approaches appealed to me and the thought of both of them together was beyond consideration. But still this article stuck in the back of a magazine I would never usually read became my first source of hope in years.

The flight, which had begun in total despondency, had suddenly brightened my entire outlook, my future, my life. My battle would no longer be an exercise in futility. At last my formidable foe had been identified. Until now I had been fighting an unseen, unknown phantom. I had been boxing at shadows, perceiving my parents as persecutors and innocent mealtime circumstances as hideously orchestrated attacks. Finally, I could see my enemy as an entity; I could call it by name and seek out weapons with which to wage war against it.

In spite of my new surge of optimism and motivation I remained strangely powerless in my struggles. I had another extensive series of medical tests run and even had a counseling session with a psychologist, but there was no resolution, no enlightenment.

There was no effective strategy developed, nor could there be with our professional demands consistently taking us from city to city. My discouragement intensified as I realized that all the weapons in the world are useless without the proper ammunition.

Although my weight had risen above the critical level to a lean but passable 105 pounds, I was still miserable inside, still driven, obsessed, captive. In many ways, this stage of my illness was even harder than those preceding it because I appeared so much better, yet I felt more desperate and drained than ever.

I was on an emotional roller coaster, the highs getting higher, the lows increasingly lower, and the extremes occurring in much greater frequency. I had opened myself up to two relationships with young men I had met, but they had ended disastrously: the first was concluded by mutual agreement while the second man left me suddenly ignored and rejected with no explanation or even a goodbye. The depression that followed was devastating. In all of my previous involvements I had done the rejecting. This time the combination of my new pain with the continued frustration of the anorexia left me feeling that I was on the brink of a complete emotional collapse. It was at this point, at twenty years of age and teetering on the edge of a nervous breakdown, that I met Dan O'Neill.

September 13, 1974. I climbed out of the swimming pool

having completed my regular daily workout and entered the sauna. I knew I was a little behind schedule but I wasn't overly concerned about being late for an appointment that had virtually been arranged for me in spite of my obvious reluctance. I reviewed the circumstances that led to this meeting as the beads of sweat grew on my skin.

When my mother's friend called, we had just returned from a lengthy summer concert tour and, with only two weeks before our next trip, we were relieved to have some time off at home. I was particularly thankful to be back so I could recuperate from my recent rejection and regain some semblance of routine and control in my life, if only for two weeks.

Then came the phone call. Apparently, some young man had just returned from the Middle East, where he had been living for fourteen months. He was temporarily staying in their home on his way to see his family in the state of Washington. That Sunday evening he had spoken in their church and she was impressed with him and his knowledge of Mid-East politics, the Hebrew language, his experiences living on a kibbutz during the infamous 1973 October War, and his insights into Judaism as the root of the Christian faith. Because she knew that I had developed an interest in the Middle East and was studying Hebrew at U.C.L.A., she felt that I ought to meet this well-traveled houseguest of hers. Jerusalem had been his last stop in a string of overseas experiences—Africa and Europe had been home for over a year prior to his working as a volunteer on two kibbutzim. She was certain that our mutual interests would stir immediate curiosity on my part to meet him before he had to leave town a week later.

My reaction was far from what she had anticipated. I was exhausted, not looking forward to inconveniences or interruptions for a while. Meeting a man was the last thing I wanted to do. I had almost decided to opt for the single life at that point and the thought of having to put on the front of a happy, stylish young woman in order to make a positive first impression on anybody, male or female, was not a part of my plan for relaxation and escape from responsibilities.

I told both her and my mom that I really wasn't interested—not right now, anyway. I tried to let her down gently because she was so enthusiastic about the potential for interaction between us. My mother had caught some of her friend's excitement and despite my protests, I agreed to a meeting set for the next afternoon. When I was told later that our friend's son would be bringing Dan O'Neill to the house at four o'clock the following day, I was still perturbed that my wishes had been overruled. And yet, I was a bit curious about him.

Ironically, I learned months later that Dan was not impressed with coming to Pat Boone's house, was unaware that he had any daughters, and was as uninterested in females as I was in males. A few days after our meeting he actually participated in a panel debate on the pros and cons of celibacy—on the pro side! He was curious about my Hebrew studies as I was about his experiences, but both of us, for our own personal reasons, were dragging our heels to our initial introduction.

I was putting the finishing touches on my hair and makeup when the doorbell rang. I rushed around, putting on my blouse, slipping into my slacks and was spraying my fresh curls into place when Lindy came in to inform me that the two young gentlemen were waiting downstairs in the recreation room. "He's really good-looking, Cherry," she added, smiling impishly. She had recently become engaged to be married so I knew her evaluation was for my benefit only.

At long last I descended the stairs and made my grand entrance at least fifteen minutes late. I was introduced to Dan O'Neill and our first words to one another were in Hebrew. As we spoke, my mind registered a confirmation of Lindy's initial description: with his deeply tanned skin and thick, wavy, sun-bleached blond hair that just teased the tops of his shoulders, he was visually striking. His pastel sweater enhanced the intense, fiery blue of his eyes. He was not particularly tall—about five foot nine. With my heeled shoes I was as tall as he. However, in spite of his medium frame and quiet demeanor, I sensed an inner strength I had never encountered in a young man.

We discussed many of our common interests through the course of the late afternoon and evening as the three of us went for dinner at a nearby restaurant. After judiciously weighing the menu's options, I decided on a chef salad with herb dressing. After all, I had completed all of my exercises and this was my first food of the day. My choice would not necessarily betray my enigmatic approach to eating. I didn't realize my systematized dining methods and extremely thin, bony wrists and fingers would suggest the existence of some puzzling problems in my life.

During our meal I discovered that Dan was a graphic designer, having graduated with a Bachelor of Fine Arts degree from the University of Washington. He was considering the possibility of finding some temporary employment with a publishing company as an illustrator while he took a leave of absence from his work overseas. I had artistic leanings myself and had contemplated creating my own illustrations to accompany a children's story called "The First Butterfly," which I had written and intended to submit for publication. Interestingly, we had both been negotiating with the same publisher. We decided to make my children's project a joint effort, since Dan's trained graphic ability would obviously exceed my amateur attempts.

The evening ended early with my two escorts proceeding on to another appointment; but Dan and I agreed to meet again in one week when he returned from a conference in Desert Hot Springs. At that time I would view his slides from the Middle East and we would go over the story I had written to discuss the style of illustration to be used and the number of drawings needed. This intriguing, talented stranger and I had suddenly become partners. I was excited about our joint venture as I watched them drive away.

When the week had passed, Dan returned to the Boone house in Beverly Hills for his second visit, slides in hand. Late again, I greeted him in the front hallway and we began a meeting that started at ten o'clock in the morning and lasted until ten o'clock that night. Neither of us planned it that way. It just happened.

After we looked at Dan's pictures, many of which included the frightful scenes of the October 1973 Middle East war and its aftermath, we moved on to the next item on our agenda. We divided my story into segments and decided that we would need ten illustrations of various caterpillars and butterflies to help in telling the tale, with an extra one to use on the cover of the book. With our business completed, I graciously prepared and served lunch to my guest, while politely abstaining. I suppose I made some feeble excuse about having had something earlier. I was careful to cook a meal he had described as one of his favorites, a four-egg mushroom omelette with a salad consisting of diced onion, cucumber, and tomato. Although I prided myself on willpower and the ability to forgo even the tiniest taste of food while creating in the kitchen, my love-hate relationship with food had led me into lengthy studies of recipes and a rather highly developed culinary expertise. Dan was duly impressed and subsequently sated as I sat and watched him enjoy his lunch, sipping on a sugar-free soda.

Our conversation continued throughout the meal and beyond, until somehow, mysteriously, I let my ever-present guard down and allowed myself to become vulnerable to this strong and friendly acquaintance. In a discussion of spiritual issues, I confessed to Dan my tentative approach to God—the result of increasing emotional instability, with my ups and downs having become even more intense in recent weeks. As if to emphasize and demonstrate my self-revelation, tears filled my eyes and overflowed, staining my cheeks and punctuating my penitential disclosure. I did not go so far as to share the gory details of my dilemma, but I was still amazed at the degree of openness with which I exposed my soul and its seemingly interminable torture. I was even more amazed by the supportive and concerned response I received in exchange for my sorrowful exposé. Although we were both speaking in somewhat vague generalities, he was acknowledging my emotional problems as real and valid, regardless of their cause, and he admitted to having discerned the presence of anxiety in my life at our first meeting. He encouraged me to stop striving to accomplish so much, to concentrate not on "doing," but on "being." He supported my idea that moving out of my parents' house and into an apartment would probably be helpful, and stressed the importance of seeking a deeper relationship with God. When I expressed doubts about my ability to follow his advice, he suggested that we pray together about my situation.

I had prayed with many different people already, including parents, pastors, friends, and other such understandably concerned parties. But rarely had I prayed with someone I did not know—and never about my own problems. I had never met someone near my own age who had such wisdom, peace, strength of character, spiritual commitment, and integrity. He had nothing to gain by laying his faith "on the line" in praying for me; he had no obligation to me whatsoever. I was so moved by his suggestion and so convinced that his prayer would be heard that I readily agreed.

I had long since abandoned the idea of an instantaneous cure or a sudden miraculous healing. I had been disappointed too many times to believe in that kind of a solution. But somewhere deep inside I still nurtured a seed of faith, however minuscule, that there was an answer, a happy ending to all the struggles.

Dan prayed and I mustered all the positive anticipation I could that this prayer would be different. Even as he spoke, I sensed that it was. I felt something inside of me well up with excitement at the thought that this could be the beginning of a real change, maybe even a lasting change. It was almost as though my spirit was holding its breath, afraid to exhale and extinguish the small, flickering flame of hope being fanned by Dan's faith.

When he finished his prayer, we looked at one another with an awareness that something unique had transpired. As I looked at him, still trying to fathom the full portent of the experience we had just shared, an unexpected, unsolicited, and even confusing thought went through my mind: "I wish I could look into those eyes for the rest of my life."

It seemed so shockingly out of context, and so foreign to

1954—our first family
Christmas.

Daddy with Arthur Godfrey—a career is born.

Elvis and Daddy comparing their blue suede and white bucks.

"Daddy Pat Boone" with Paul Anka, Frankie Avalon, Bobby Darin—the gold records kept on coming.

An intimate moment shared by Daddy and daughter.

Our family show-biz debut on the final episode of Daddy's "Chevy Showroom" TV series (*left to right:* Mommy, Debby, Lindy, me, Laury, Daddy).

One of the hundreds of poses for family photos (*left to right:* Cherry, Pat, Lindy, Shirley, Debby, Laury).

The Boone family arrives in Hollywood to a warm fan club welcome (*left to right:* Shirley, Laury, Debby, Pat, Lindy, Cherry).

When food meant family fun (*left to right:* Cherry, Shirley, Lindy).

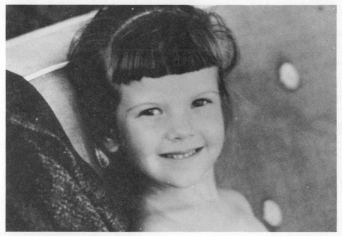

Smiles came naturally to this carefree five-year-old.

From the beginning I worked hard to "make the grade."

Playing piano for my childhood heartthrob, Ed "Kookie" Byrnes, one of the stars of "77 Sunset Strip."

Plump and insecure at age 13.

A surprise nighttime birthday party for Mommy—Osmonds and Boones harmonize a birthday song (*left to right:* Jay, Marie, Merrill, Lindy, Laury, Alan, Donny, Wayne, Cherry, Debby).

Another family photo—and striving for perfection at age 14 (*left to right:* Cherry, Shirley, Lindy, Pat, Debby, Laury).

At age 18. Family funning hides my deepening emotional crisis (*left to right:* Cherry, Shirley, Lindy, Pat, Laury, Debby).

Helping to prepare a meal I wouldn't eat (*left to right:* Laury, Cherry, Shirley, Lindy, Debby).

Singing at seventeen: an album (and an anoretic) in the making.

Christmas carols with Glen Campbell (*left to right:* Cherry, Laury, Lindy, Glen, Debby).

Family fun on Flip Wilson's TV show, 1971 (*left to right:* Pat, Shirley, Cherry, Lindy, Flip, Debby, Laury).

The Boones with Mike Douglas, 1972 (*left to right:* Laury, Shirley, Debby, Mike, Lindy, Pat, Cherry).

A brief chat with Henry Kissinger after our Kennedy Center performance, 1972.

Boones and Nixons—an Oval Office visit (*left to right:* Cherry, Lindy, Debby, Laury, President Nixon, Pat, Shirley, Mrs. Nixon).

Daddy and daughter—a commercial poster marketed in Japan, 1974.

October 4, 1975, Dan and I were married.

Al Panzieri

Skin and bone—I thought I was too heavy.

At 88 pounds, I scavenged the remains of a turkey carcass—a rare photo from the famine years.

Moments before our first session with Dr. Vath, and straining to smile—I weighed 82 pounds.

With good friends, the Ganfields—I was 89 pounds, but gaining.

Dancing toward health with Hudson brothers in Boone family TV special, 1978 (*left to right:* Cherry, Bill, Debby, Mark, Lindy, Brett, Laury).

On the mend in Hawaii, Thanksgiving Day, 1978, with special friends (*left to right:* Owenses, Hamptons, O'Neills, Kerrs, Boones).

Happy and healthy with husband, Dan, and daughter, Brittany, 1982.

A recent "Boone Girls" album—we still sing. Tunes are happier today.

Brittany riding high.

David Barnes

A happy family feeding time.

David Barnes

David Barnes

A quiet moment with
Brittany in a contemplative
mood.

Pint-size pianist—I took my performing seriously.

Making music once again.

David Barnes

my other thoughts that I dismissed it immediately as a misplaced intrusion on this almost transcendental moment.

Suddenly, Dan and I both realized that our uninterrupted gaze into one another's eyes had endured beyond the point of propriety into the realm of awkwardness and even slight embarrassment. As magically as it had emerged, it disappeared and the spell was broken. Nevertheless, we both knew that something indescribable had taken place, something extraordinary and uncommon.

Dan had dinner with the whole family that evening and after casual conversation continuing into the night, he finally left for Shelton, Washington, to stay with his family for a while. As for me, the encounter touched off an emotional high that lasted through the next few weeks. It was like sailing on a cloud—a cloud, I thought, that might just have a silver lining. Circumstances, details, and even dreams seemed to be coming together in a way that confirmed an intuitive suspicion that my emancipation had commenced. In fact, I was so enthused over this chain of events and so convinced of their significance that I actually sat down and listed them all, describing even the dreams and their symbolic meanings in a letter to Dan. Although it looked more like a novel than an epistle, I felt he ought to know about the fireworks ignited by his spark of faith. It was as if I was sending him my "liberation papers" in thanks for the role he played in my emerging freedom. Ironically, he still had not been informed about the horrible, monstrous skeleton lurking in my secret closet.

Our communication picked up both through the mail and over the phone. We were anticipating the presentation of our collaborative publishing effort to the president of the company we had selected, and I used our joint project as an excuse to maintain contact with my new friend and confidant. We planned a trip for Dan to Los Angeles in early December, at which time he would stay in our guest house and we would have our eagerly awaited meeting with the publisher.

Along with our long-distance professional discussions I shared news of continuing improvements and hopeful signs in my personal life. My latest medical checkup had positive results. Even the dentist had reported that the enamel erosion had apparently ceased. We had every indication that the nightmare might indeed be coming to an end.

It was in this atmosphere of joyful expectancy that failure occurred. Just when I thought I had outrun my tenacious pursuer, there was a head-on collision. It happened again— from kitchen to toilet. Distraught and disillusioned, I recoiled at my mother's suggestion that I call and ask Dan for help. How could I admit such blatant weakness to someone so strong and so disciplined, especially after the several successes I had related only days earlier? The mere thought of it sickened me. But Mommy persuaded me and I seated myself at an extension phone as she dialed the phone on her night table. I picked up the receiver and listened.

"I have a person-to-person call for a Dan O'Neill from Beverly Hills, California," the operator monotoned.

"Oh!" A surprised but pleasant voice inquired politely, "May I ask who is calling?"

"Shirley Boone is calling long distance for a Mr. Dan O'Neill."

"One moment, please," the unidentified voice requested, sounding slightly puzzled.

As I waited for Dan to take his call, the silence seemed to shout at me, "Hang up! Get off now while you still can!" And yet as much as I dreaded divulging my downfall, I still felt that somehow, mysteriously, Dan could provide me with the stepping stones to health. I squirmed in my chair as I thought about the shame of admitting defeat to someone whom I respected so highly. But it was too late. My options disappeared as the phone was picked up on the other end of the line.

"Dan O'Neill speaking."

"Dan, this is Shirley Boone, Cherry's mother."

"Oh, Mrs. Boone! Hello," Dan responded tentatively, confused at hearing Mommy's voice and wondering about the reason for this unusual call.

"I'm calling about Cherry, Dan. She's on the phone with me and we just felt she should talk to you because . . . well, she's been having some problems again."

I cringed.

"What kind of problems?" he asked.

"Oh, the same as usual. But she'd been doing so well, making such progress and then all of a sudden it all started to surface again. She's really been upset, Dan, and since you helped her so much before, we thought you might have some words of wisdom or some insights to encourage her now."

"Well, Mrs. Boone," Dan answered in bewilderment, "I'm not sure I understand what has happened."

"Cherry, do you want to share with Dan . . . ?" my mom prompted.

No, I don't, my mind screamed.

"I just don't understand it, Dan!" I began to cry. "It seemed like everything was under control, like I was really getting better, but now it's like nothing ever changed! I'm right back where I was when I started!" I cleared my throat in an attempt to dispel the lump welling up inside. Fighting back the tears, I continued to try to explain in the most ambiguous terms that my "new freedom" had not, in fact, taken hold.

Dan felt as though he were being approached as some spiritual medicine man, and he did not appreciate the subtle pressure of having to come up with some instant answers. How could he evaluate any problem so vague and undefined as this? However, he took a valiant stab at it and somehow managed to comfort me, reassure my mother, and commit himself to moral support in the future. When we hung up I felt as if I had someone much stronger than I fighting in my corner. With new resolve and rising motivation I determined once again to attain victory over my persistent foe.

The December meeting came and went, and our children's book was to be considered for publication. But more importantly, the week Dan was our houseguest proved a wonderful opportunity for our friendship to flower. We spent almost every waking moment together, talking, sharing, discovering how many common interests we had. We ate together, walked together, jogged together, fasted together (both of us had developed the habit of abstaining from food for one day out of every week—the same day, at that).

Towards the end of the week, after having dinner at the home of some friends the day before Dan was scheduled to return to Washington, a surprising and unexpected phenomenon took place. The young, zealous, disciplined Dan O'Neill, having braced his heart against the onslaught of feminine arrows aimed at winning his affections (to the point of seeming like an iceberg to most members of the opposite sex), finally noticed that I was female. And not an unattractive one, at that. The frozen chamber that had kept his emotions hidden safe and inaccessible was slowly melting.

I could feel the warmth in his gaze as we talked in the kitchen by the dim light of the stove lamp. To my amazement, and pleasure, he kissed me on the cheek before retiring to the guest house. When I took him to the airport the following afternoon, we kissed each other goodbye. That morning he had offered a casual invitation to come up to Shelton to stay at his parents' home for a visit. I intended to take him up on the offer as soon as possible. I knew something special was brewing between us.

It did not take me long to find a hole in my schedule to fly up to Washington to see Dan and meet his family. Exactly one month from the time he had departed Los Angeles, I was on my way up to Seattle. The fact that I was taking my very first trip alone at age twenty seemed a bit strange considering the miles I had logged as a traveler, but I was excited about what unknown possibilities awaited me at my destination. I had agreed to sing at a few church-related functions where Dan would be speaking, but beyond that the course that lay ahead was completely uncharted. This was truly to be an adventure!

During the four days of my visit, I not only met many of Dan's friends and family, all of whom I liked immediately, but we continued to develop the many facets of our deepening relationship. It was becoming apparent to both of us that friendship had given way to a full-blown romance. Neither of us had pursued that kind of involvement but there it was, real and alive. We were both swept away in the rushing tide of new love and new life. We were enjoying it, and one another, thoroughly.

One night as we were returning from our last church engagement, I was hit with the realization that if this relationship was to continue, Dan deserved to know the truth about my problems and my practices, no matter what the cost. With every ounce of courage I could marshal, I related to him the unpleasant details of my anorexia from its inception to the state of semicontrol I felt I currently had over it. I told him about my obsessions with food, diet, and exercise; my fear of gaining weight; the binges, vomiting, abuse of laxatives, shoplifting—I laid it all out like a sickening mural of assorted neuroses painted on the backdrop of an otherwise carefree life. The whole sordid mess was finally revealed; the monster had been unveiled.

I held my breath as I waited for Dan's response to my disgusting divulgence. To my relief and utter amazement, his reaction was incredibly mild. In fact, he never flinched during the telling of my horror story and, upon its conclusion, he unhesitatingly avowed his unfaltering support for me. He assured me that the two of us, working together, could conquer this menace I had been battling for so long. Honesty had most certainly been the best policy and a wise decision after all. Dan's love and acceptance of me appeared to be unchanged by my revelations. Obviously, he had known that I was having some severe emotional problems when we met and it was obvious that I was underweight. At our first meeting he had remembered seeing what he described as a "jewelry-draped skeleton," complete with all the essential Beverly Hills externals while physically, psychologically, and spiritually I was barely alive. He had guessed that my secret struggles somehow involved food and weight.

Feeling Dan's supportiveness and love in the face of my full confession was one of the most refreshing and encouraging surprises I could ever have hoped to receive. He knew it all, yet he still cared for me. How could that be? In spite of all the failures and inadequacies, he still loved me, still wanted me. More than ever, I felt compelled to vanquish the enemy of my life, for his sake, if not mine. He deserved a healthy, happy fulfilled person in his life and I was resolute in my determination that he would have nothing less. Heaving a huge sigh of relief and feeling that the burden of my secret life was somewhat lighter by the sharing of it, I returned home convinced that I was in love and, incredibly, that I was loved and that this love would make me well.

February brought another professional endeavor to which we were both asked to contribute. Although we received our invitations to assist in a tour of the Middle East independently of one another, the source of the invitations was none other than the mutual friends who had instigated our introduction in September. Dan was to help in leading the tour group and I was to prepare music to teach to the travelers on their pilgrimage to the Holy Land. Once again, it afforded us an opportunity to be together and Dan decided to come down to Los Angeles early to coordinate last minute details. He would stay with us for several days prior to our departure.

Dan arrived on Valentine's Day and that afternoon after lunch we sat together in an open meadow while we exchanged cards and admissions of past failures and regretted relationships. I experienced new depths of emotion for Dan as he confided in me mistakes he had made before we met. Even in his confession of guilt and subsequent remorse, I saw strength of character I had never seen in the young men I had dated. Dan O'Neill was my tower of strength—a paragon, a pillar on which I could lean in my moments of weakness. The fact that he actually loved me enough to trust me with his own humanness seemed too good to be true.

Two days later on a long drive on the sunny California

coast, one of the most wonderful events of my life took place. We parked the car on a bluff overlooking the wide expanse of ocean below. The blue of the sea and the blue of the sky merged on the horizon and appeared to become one. It was as if God Himself had orchestrated His natural creation to set the scene for what was about to occur. There on that hilltop and in that absolutely idyllic setting, Dan told me that he felt God wanted us to be married. He didn't ask me; he didn't really have to. I had been dreaming about this moment for weeks and my dream was coming true. While we embraced and watched the sunset, the whole world exploded into brilliant colors as the sun stooped to kiss both sea and sky at their point of oneness. I saw it as a sacrament of God's blessing, confirming our union. It would be an uncommon, yes, even perfect marriage. All of nature was singing in joyous agreement.

With the happy consent of my surprised father (Mommy had been apprised of the relationship's development at every stage) and the tour behind us, we began making plans for our wedding. The date was to be October 4, 1975, for the convenience of our pastor, and so that my summer obligations to perform with the family would already be fulfilled. The fact that we would be preceding Lindy's nuptial ceremony by eight weeks precipitated some sibling resentment, but together the brides, grooms, and parents of the brides-to-be resolved the potential conflict.

I was given my engagement ring during an April visit to Shelton with my parents so that the prospective in-laws could meet. Shortly thereafter, Dan moved down to Los Angeles where he began working as an editor for a publishing company. Dan's proximity not only facilitated the organization of our wedding, but it enabled us to spend much more time together. In spite of the professional demands on both of us, we managed to spend most of our leisure time together. We designed our invitations and announcements, addressed them together, registered for dishes, silverware, and linens, chose furniture for our apartment, and somehow we managed an occasional dinner or movie.

As exhilarated as I was about my future, my past was still nipping at my heels. Although Dan was there to help and encourage me, I still occasionally yielded to the old temptations as they moved against me with a kind of relentless power. Granted, my failures were fewer and less frequent. I was eating more regularly and trying to avoid delicacies which could trigger a binge. But still there were moments when the pressures of working, arranging a large wedding, and trying to maintain an ongoing romantic relationship weighed heavily on me.

When I would relax my vigilance, the "demons" that haunted me would rear their ugly heads and attack at my weakest point. I was no longer emaciated; I was well above my critical weight. At about 106 pounds I was actually starting to look quite healthy. Even my menstrual cycle spontaneously resumed shortly after my first trip to Seattle. On the exterior everything appeared to be in order. But in the quiet of my room, behind my bathroom door, locked securely to protect me from intruders, I perpetuated my ritual purging practices after swallowing mountains of food and drink. I felt I had successfully conquered my weight problem, and yet despite daily attempts and repeated promises to myself and to God, I still could not control this one remaining habit.

Dan knew that I was still struggling but I could not bring myself to inform him of the full extent of my failures. I did not want to lose him now, so close to our wedding day.

Besides, I could handle this one last manifestation on my own, I kept telling myself. I can get myself back in control. I allowed myself to tell him that I was afraid I might be eating too much. After all, following years of bizarre eating behavior I no longer felt I really knew what was normal. I tried to rely on his input to apply boundaries to my neurotic extremism.

One night, after a full dinner at a nice restaurant, Dan delivered me to my doorstep. As we said goodnight, he warned me not to give in to any temptations to nibble my way to bed.

"Now just go right through that kitchen and upstairs to your room. You had plenty to eat for dinner and you don't need anything else, okay?"

"Did I eat too much tonight?" I asked with obvious insecurity.

"No, I don't think you ate too much, but you did have a substantial amount. And that's good! But you need to draw the line. You've had a healthy meal and now it's time to sleep. Now, promise me you'll go straight to bed. No more food."

"I promise," I answered, sincerely believing that I would not betray Dan's trust.

"Okay, good! I'll see you tomorrow night then. I love you." He kissed me goodnight.

"I love you, too," I said as I waved and closed the back door. I turned around to do Dan's bidding when my eyes fell on a mound of leftover meat scraps in Summa's dog dish. They had lamb chops tonight, I thought to myself, realizing I'd missed my favorite dinner. Suddenly, the kitchen's lingering aroma wafted its way into my nostrils and the image of the savory, glistening fat and the thought of the juicy marrow resting in the bone overwhelmed me. I couldn't stand the idea of those delectable morsels going to the dog. Without thinking, in the shadows of the laundry room between the back door and kitchen, I impulsively squatted to the floor to feast on the dinner's remnants.

I started slowly, relishing the flavor and texture of each marvelous bite. Soon I was ripping the meager remains from the bones, stuffing the cold meat into my mouth as fast as I could detach it. Suddenly, I heard a rap on the window behind me. I spun around to see who it was.

Oh my God, no! It was Dan! He was standing at the back door watching me. There was a look of horror, disbelief, and total disgust on his face. I had been caught red-handed in the betrayal of his trust, in the breaking of my promise, in an animalistic orgy on the floor, in the dark, alone. Here was the horrid truth for Dan to see. I felt so evil, tainted, pagan.

Trembling, I stood up and opened the door.

"What do you think you are doing?" Dan asked incredulously.

"I'm . . . I . . . there was . . ." I sputtered nonsense, searching madly for a reasonable explanation. There was none, and I knew it.

"Do I *know* you? Do I even know you at *all?* Who *are* you anyway? Doesn't your word mean *anything?*" Dan's questions came at me like knives piercing my heart. I dissolved into tears.

"I'm sorry, Dan! I don't know what happened! I really meant it when I promised I'd go to bed, honest. But then I saw the lamb chops. I didn't mean to blow it, Dan. I'm sorry, really!" I apologized profusely between sobs.

"Eating cold, leftover meat out of the dog's dish after you gave me your word that you would go straight to bed. I just can't believe it! It's disgusting!"

"Dan, please, I'm sorry!" I cried hysterically.

"I have to go. I can't handle this. Goodnight!" Dan turned and started to leave.

"Are you still going to come over tomorrow night?" I asked, pleading hopefully.

He never stopped to turn around. But I heard his answer as he disappeared from view into the inky darkness of the night.

"I don't know."

Never before and never since have I experienced the depths of depression and utter despair that I felt during the next twenty-four-hour period. After watching Dan walk away from me, possibly forever for all I knew, I collapsed in a heap of moaning and tears. Sackcloth and ashes would have seemed like party hats and confetti to me at that moment. I was mourning the death of our relationship, the death of my honor, of my self-respect—the death of hope. Everything looked bleak and I felt like I was trapped in some sadistic cosmic nightmare—a surreal, inner twilight zone where nothing made sense. The full weight of my actions came crashing down on me like the gates of hell itself. I felt alienated from Dan, disillusioned with myself, and separated from God. It was truly my own personal "dark night of the soul."

The following day was not much better. The burden of my sins was so heavy that I felt physically weak from shouldering them all night long. In spite of the fact that the family was scheduled to tape a television commercial that day, I could barely stand up, let alone eat, drink, or talk. With puffy eyes and rubbery legs I performed my professional duties, but with every opportunity I returned to a sitting or reclining position. Just being alive seemed like an awful chore. Everything around me became frivolous and extraneous invasions into my mental preoccupations with the stark realities of good and evil.

When we returned to the house that evening I buried myself in a book called *God's Chosen Fast,* about the proper spiritual and biblical approach to food. My yellow-ink pen colored nearly every paragraph as I underlined important passages and made personal notes in the margin.

Then, unexpectedly, Dan arrived. I was at once pleasantly surprised and shamefully humiliated. On the one hand I desired an opportunity to express to Dan my total remorse and repentance, and yet on the other hand I was embarrassed to show my face to him. My mother preceded Dan into my bedroom and perched herself on the side of my bed where I lay on my stomach studying my book. Dan followed her in and sat on a chair across from me as I shared the desperation that had been plaguing me.

Dan had taken the incident seriously, even personally. It was a revelation to him of my true character, or lack of it. It had affected his feelings towards me and the change was painfully evident. Mommy tried to soften Dan's dissertation on the consequences of my choices by inserting comments about God's grace. She had seen too many suicidal personalities to take my depression lightly. And yet, I tended to agree with Dan's point of view: what I had done was awful, ugly, and hurtful. My repentance would have to bear the fruit of a changed life before I could expect to be restored to a full relationship with both Dan and God. I promised both of them that the effects of the previous night's events would resonate within my soul as a force moving me towards righteousness from that moment on. Over dinner that evening I felt more sure than ever that my priorities had at last been properly and permanently set. Dan, however, would never fully trust me again. His doubts would linger for years as a result of that one rueful, loathsome night.

Happily, our wedding plans continued. As the day approached, my condition improved steadily and both Dan and I eagerly anticipated the coming union. Everything was organized, all the details were attended to, and Dan had accepted the idea that our ceremony would inevitably be a media event. He disliked the idea that we could not have a normal, quiet, private wedding like everyone else, but Mommy and I explained to him that we had lived public lives and the people out there, the fans and magazine readers, would want to see photographs and read about Pat Boone's daughter getting married. Finally, we struck a compromise that both Dan and my parents could live with: the photographers could pounce on us only as we left the church to get into Daddy's Rolls-Royce for the drive to our Bel-Air Country Club reception. There would be no press photographers inside during the ceremony (only one authorized by us for our own records) and, to my parents' chagrin, Dan vetoed the videotaping of the grand event for posterity. We wanted the experience to be imprinted on our hearts and minds—not on ferrous oxide.

The wedding came off without a hitch. Debby and Daddy sang their songs beautifully, the dresses and tuxedos were tailored exquisitely, the floral archway over the altar was elegant, the church was full of friends and relatives, and Daddy wasn't late for the ceremony. (Knowing his predisposition for tardiness, we decided to take our pictures *before* the wedding.) Our pastor, Jack Hayford, spoke eloquently about marriage in general and ours specifically. He compared it to a fine wine that improves with age and confirmed to us and the company in attendance what Dan and I already believed in our hearts—that ours would be an uncommon union, an ideal example of marriage for all to behold.

When he pronounced us man and wife, we emerged from the sanctuary onto the front steps of the church feeling that a new life had indeed come into the world. And as expected, cameras clicked and flashbulbs popped as we made our way to the two-toned convertible Rolls that sat at the curb with Daddy poised at the wheel ready to whisk us away to make our official debut as Mr. and Mrs. D. O'Neill.

The wedding was wonderful and the honeymoon ever more so . . . until we bought a laxative to encourage my sluggish intestines to function properly. That simple purchase began another chain of abusive, weight-reducing behaviors and by the time we returned to our apartment to begin our life of wedded bliss, I was back to all of my old tricks, including secrecy.

For ten weeks, I succeeded in hiding the truth from Dan. I wasn't exercising anymore. I had carefully scheduled my time to incorporate the many new household chores I had never regularly done before. What leisure time remained proved to be "the devil's playground." The binges and subsequent vomiting were becoming habitual again, as was overdosing on laxatives. Fortunately, there was little leisure time because of concert tours to rehearse for, fittings for new costumes, and an album to record. But I always found time to gorge and purge myself whenever I wanted.

One night while driving home from a late-night recording session, I stopped at several all-night food stores and ate doughnuts, a burrito, a cheeseburger, and brownies, washing it all down with two milkshakes. A block from our apartment, with Dan in bed waiting for me to arrive home, I pulled into an alleyway to relieve myself of both my physical discomfort and my guilt. When I climbed into bed

I told Dan that a wrong exit on the freeway had caused me to be late.

One would have to have been blind not to have noticed the drastic drop in my weight. Ten pounds had been shed in less than six weeks and on the day of Lindy's wedding, November 29, 1975, I looked in the mirror and gasped. For once, even I could readily see that the image reflected in the glass was cadaverous. I actually scared myself as I examined my bony face, arms, and shoulders. What a difference from my wedding photos taken only eight weeks before!

The next two weeks were torture for me. I knew I needed help but I was still denying to everyone, including Dan, that I had a problem. I was becoming edgy, irritable, and emotionally frayed and my new husband was wondering if he had been deceived. I was certainly not the same young bride he had taken just two months earlier, and he was letting me know about it. It was apparent to him that something was drastically wrong and getting worse.

On a cool, crisp Sunday afternoon in December I informed Dan that I needed to talk with him. We had been to church together that morning and the sermon had convinced me of my need to be completely honest with Dan. Confident that I was doing the right thing I courageously clasped his hand as we walked to a nearby park. There I proceeded to bare my soul to him, sure that he would be proud of me for confessing and would accept me lovingly as he had that first time I openly shared the reality of my anorexia with him. I disclosed the details of my downfall during our honeymoon and brought him up to date with stories of recent defeats in my battle with the same unrelenting obsessions.

When I had finished calmly revealing the previously

hidden and even outrightly denied foibles, I waited for Dan's strong supportive arms to encircle me like a harbor of safety from my own internal storms and for his congratulations for wisely choosing the course of total transparency.

My plan backfired! Instead of Dan's love covering my multitude of sins, I felt him draw away from me—a cold, steel barrier instantly materialized between us. Rejection! Was that my reward for honesty? It was all so confusing.

Dan was cut to the quick. He had been betrayed! Were my marriage vows meaningless? Was our marriage a mockery? What about all those glowing promises? Wasn't it bad enough that I had done these awful things without adding insult to injury by concealing and denying them? Why had I waited so long to tell him? Telling him that he had been deceived was sufficiently traumatic without rubbing salt in the wounds by informing him that the cover-up had been going on for two months. In Dan's mind that day, I had been whoring after food, and worse, violating his trust and our relationship by lying. When we returned to our apartment, I was devastated. Once he had expressed his feelings, he retreated into silence—a reaction that frightened me. If we couldn't communicate, how would the breach between us be repaired? I cried, I begged, I pleaded with him—still not a word. It was as if he was in a state of emotional shock. Ironically, my attempt at total honesty had been to Dan an admission of total dishonesty.

With her usual impeccable timing, my mother showed up at our door with a couple of milkshakes. She knew immediately that she had stumbled into an emotional mine field. Dan's somber expression and my swollen, tear-tracked face were unmistakable. In vague terms we described what had happened and she excused herself, feeling that three was definitely a crowd. Dan walked her to her car where Mommy warned him to be easy on me and elaborated on my suicidal symptoms.

"She's got more sense than that!" Dan's retort shot back.

"Just be careful, Dan. She's so sensitive." As Mommy got in the car and drove away, she was as fearful of the latent rage she sensed in Dan as she was of my own self-destructiveness.

Later, when Dan finally began speaking to me again, I begged him to help me.

"I'll do *anything* you say—*anything!*" I announced resolutely. I had to, because I had long since run out of ideas of my own and I had nothing else from which to draw. So, at Dan's prompting, we drew up a regimented eating plan that deliberately excluded any foods that had prompted my binges. Everything with sugar and almost everything with flour except for an occasional piece of whole-wheat toast was eliminated. I followed it with a vengeance, and when my parents gave me a membership at a local health spa, I felt like I finally had my life under control once again.

Meanwhile, I was trying to learn how to be a homemaker and, although I had gotten off to a good start, I was frustrated that my shopping, cooking, cleaning, washing, ironing, vacuuming, and dusting schedule was being ruined by any number of outside obligations. I was still contracted to be on the road with my family thirty days out of the year, which did not include business meetings, rehearsals, fittings, recording, local performances, and television productions. When I wasn't involved professionally with the rest of the clan, I was involved personally or socially. In fact, it appeared to Dan that I was spending at least one third of my life on the phone with Mommy. Needless to say, my loyalties were being challenged. Yes, I was now Mrs. Dan O'Neill, but on stage I was still expected to be a "Boone girl''—happy, smiling, talented, and definitely problem-free. Where did Boone end and O'Neill begin? Where did Cherry fit in, if at all? Did Cherry even really exist? Had she ever? Who is she?

At the same time, Dan was under extreme pressure at his office. His job was demanding and he seemed to be saddled with the work of at least four people. His boss was a superachiever who expected his employees to be equally productive. (Daddy recently likened working for this gentleman to planning Armageddon during a lunch break!) The stress of Dan's job was taking its own toll.

In mid-March we returned from our second tour to the Holy Land headed by Dan's boss. This one had been with eight times as many people as before—921 to be exact. While we were there I was unable to continue my strict diet and exercise program which had successfully kept me at 113 incident-free pounds. There was no gorging or vomiting for more than three months. Often we would be served a meal indigenous to the area and I had no way of identifying the ingredients, not to mention calories. On other occasions, the only foods available I knew contained items from my "danger list." After a few days I abandoned the rules and decided to enjoy my trip. Fresh baked bread with butter and fruit jellies, Middle Eastern pastries, Arab delicacies from the old city of Jerusalem—all of the "no-nos" I had been avoiding were suddenly accessible. When I arrived home I had gained weight and lost discipline.

I returned immediately to the health club for my Monday-Wednesday-Friday workouts, beginning with a thirty-minute personalized program designed specifically for me. Then I took a half-hour group class, followed by a swim, a whirlpool, and a steambath. But my appetite had increased over the last several weeks so I began to jog again, first on

Tuesdays and Thursdays around a five-mile course, later Monday through Saturday. Eventually, I was running the course twice on as many mornings as possible, while telling Dan I had only run five miles, or none at all.

When I failed to get my eating habits under control again, the regurgitation practices returned as a safety valve for my stomach and my emotions. Gradually, I started to withdraw again, lying, hiding, and sneaking—burying my worries beneath the anesthetizing balm of food. And then flushing them down the toilet.

Dan had come to recognize the telltale signs by now. He questioned me about some of them, but of course I assured him that I was doing fine as I looked at him with a pained expression, appalled that he would actually suspect that I was back to all of the old tricks again. With every passing day, Dan was becoming increasingly convinced that I was lying until finally he started to play the role of a detective. After trailing me on a few of my ten-mile runs and then confronting me and catching me in lies, he launched a program of full-scale espionage.

One day Dan arrived home early from work. During his lunch break several hours before he had popped into the apartment to find me huddled over a blender full of a suspicious-looking concoction. He had questioned my ability to handle something like that without it setting the binge-purge cycle in motion. I flew off the handle in a wild flurry of high-pitched, defensive declarations of innocence. He left the scene fully aware that some deep trouble was ready to erupt. So when he returned that afternoon, he was looking for any signs that might indicate that I was having problems with food again.

On a hunch he walked over to the garbage bin next to the parking garage. As he peered into it he spotted a paper bag loaded with trash that had an empty box of brown sugar on top. He knew he had seen a similar box in one of our cabinets that same day during his lunch hour. Then he reached into the bag to see what other damning evidence lurked inside: candy wrappers, ice-cream cartons, empty bags of cookies and boxes of doughnuts, a gutted chocolate-cake tin, Twinkie wrappers, and an empty box of laxatives. The evidence at hand was rather conclusive.

He walked through the door and greeted me casually. Then he asked me what I had eaten during that day.

"Well, I had melon and toast for breakfast and that blender drink for lunch, you know, the protein drink you saw me eating when you came by. It had yogurt in it and . . ."

"What about the brown sugar?" Dan asked coolly.

"What brown sugar?" My heart was in my throat as I answered innocently.

"The brown sugar in the box in the kitchen cabinet—*that* brown sugar. How much of that did you eat?" Dan's controlled exterior was suppressing his growing anger.

"Why are you asking me about the brown sugar? I didn't eat any of that!" I was baffled by his line of questioning. He had no reason to believe I'd eaten any food but that which I listed to him already.

"What about the Twinkies? How many of those did you consume today?"

"What are you talking about, Dan? I told you already—all I ate was melon, toast, and a protein drink! Why are you asking me all of this?" Fear mounted within me as I realized that somehow, mysteriously, he knew what I had done, what I had eaten! But how? There was no way! Unless he had been spying on me all day—and yet that was impossible! I called him at the office in the middle of my binge to make certain that he was busy at work and wouldn't suddenly appear at home unannounced and unexpected. I couldn't take a chance that he was merely making lucky guesses. I had to stick to my story. He may not really know anything at all.

"Are you telling me you didn't eat any ice cream, chocolate cake, candy bars, or doughnuts along with the Twinkies and brown sugar?" Dan's icy expression was melting with the rage beginning to boil inside him. He walked towards me, squinting his slate-blue eyes, defying me to lie to his face.

I was dumbfounded! He had named every item I had included in my day-long binge! How could he know? He couldn't. There was no possible way! He was bluffing—he had to be!

"No, Dan, I told you what I had! Why are you doing this to me?" I appeared offended, persecuted.

"You're lying to me!" he accused.

"No, I'm not!"

"Yes, you are. You're lying to me! Right to my face! And it doesn't even phase you! Now, are you going to tell me the truth, or not?"

"I *did* tell you the truth!" I defended, through my tears.

"You're a liar! The garbage bin was full of all your precious wrappers and you emptied the kitchen trash before the bag was even full! And what about the powdered sugar, cereal, and honey in the cabinet. Are you going to lie about that too?"

I hadn't fully recovered from being hit with the realization that Dan had hard evidence proving my uncontrolled splurge and my attempts to conceal it. And now he was firing away with more!

"I don't know what you're talking about! I didn't have

anything else. That garbage must belong to someone else! There are other people in these apartments who empty their trash in that container, you know!" I whined belligerently.

"Oh come on, Cherry! Don't be ridiculous. Now tell me about all the other stuff you vomited down the toilet today!" The accusations were increasing.

"I didn't eat anything else and I *didn't* throw up!" I began to cry uncontrollably, partly from fear, partly from guilt.

"The levels of cereal, powdered sugar, and honey in the containers all went down by a couple of inches or more! Now are you going to keep on lying to me or are you going to tell the truth?"

"You've been measuring the amounts of everything in the cabinets? Oh, Dan!"

"Well, how am I supposed to determine the truth about your food games when you're lying through your teeth? Do you expect me to go on being deceived forever. I'm not stupid, you know!"

"But Dan, that's . . ."

"That's what you get when you lie to me!" Dan flung his sunglasses into the wall, shattering them with the impact. He gritted his teeth and grabbed me by the arm, pulling me into the bedroom. I resisted his aggression at first, afraid that he might totally lose control and hurt me somehow. But his grip just tightened as he forcefully shoved me down on the bed. He picked up my purse and started to rummage through it.

"Let's see what poison you're hiding in here!" he seethed.

"What are you doing now, Dan?" I whimpered.

"What do you think I'm doing? Here—what's in here?"

He opened up a change purse I had hidden in a zippered compartment of my bag.

"Ah, yes! Here it is! Now, are you going to tell me more lies? What's this?" He held a handful of white, candy-coated pieces of gum up to my face.

"It's gum," I said. "Why?"

"What kind of gum?"

"Just regular gum! Is there something wrong with that?"

"You're lying again!" He tossed them across the room and grabbed me by the collar of my shirt, ripping a seam in the sleeve.

"Dan, don't! Please!" I didn't know what he might do.

"Stop lying to me!" He slammed my shoulders onto the bed and bounced me up and down.

"All right! All right! They're laxatives! Please! Just stop!" I was overcome with fear.

He picked up my purse, held it upside down, and shook it, emptying the contents onto the floor.

"Do you have any other little magic potions hiding in here?"

"No! No! That's all!" I sobbed.

He threw my purse so hard that it came apart as it hit the wall.

"I'm sick of your damned lies! Who the hell do you think I am anyway—some kind of mindless idiot?"

Both of us were taken aback by the sudden outburst of expletives. That kind of language had been foreign to our vocabulary—until now.

"Okay, Dan," I moaned feebly, "I had the cereal and honey and powdered sugar. I put the honey on some cereal and I added powdered sugar to my drink but I didn't have that other stuff in the garbage bin. And I didn't throw up! I swear!" I maintained as much of my original story as I thought I could still expect him to believe. After all, he had no proof that I had actually eaten those other things.

"You are incredible! You're acting like a child!" Dan's volatile eruption gave way to perplexed unbelief.

"What do you mean? I'm telling you the truth, honest!"

"Okay! You want to act like a child, you'll get treated like a child!" My lies had rekindled his rage. He pulled me across his lap and began to spank me.

When he was through I curled up on the bed and whimpered as he grabbed his keys and went for a reckless ride on his motorcycle. Both of us were in shock at what had just transpired, both of us were looking for an escape from the horror that plagued our marriage—however self-destructive that escape might be.

How had we sunk to this? What had become of that ideal "uncommon union" that would shine for all to see? Had that first prayer together in my parents' home been in vain? Had it meant nothing at all? Where was all of this leading? Where would it all end? Would there ever *be* an end?

In the throes of despair, we could see no answers. We did not know at our initial encounter that we had, in fact, begun a long arduous journey into a darkening chamber of horrors. All we knew then was that we had sunk to the depths of our own private hell.

CHAPTER SEVEN

Death Diet

"What?!" Dan rolled over and quickly sat up in bed looking back at where he had just been sleeping. He reached down to touch the wet, freshly stained sheets in an effort to determine what the source of the dark-colored dampness might be.

"Cherry, what is this?" he queried.

"Cherry!" he repeated.

Finally aroused from a comalike sleep that had come only after a fitful, restless night, I rolled over to see why Dan was making such a commotion.

"My gosh! Cherry! What's wrong with you? You look awful! What happened?" The expression of horror on Dan's face took me by surprise. Once I gathered my wits, I replied in a weak voice.

"I think I've caught your flu bug, Dan. I feel terrible. I was up in the middle of the night with diarrhea and cramps in my stomach and back—even my hands and feet were hurting."

"Your face looks like a mummy's! I can't believe the drastic change overnight! It might as well just be a skull with a thin layer of skin stretched across it! How could that happen? It didn't happen to me with my flu."

His attention returned to the soggy mattress beneath him. Suddenly the horrible reality of what had occurred hit Dan, sending a wave of disgust across his face. The sickness had attacked me with such violence that I had lost all control of my bowels.

"Oh my gosh! This mess in the bed is yours! Didn't you know what was going on? Couldn't you make it to the bathroom?" Dan was utterly repulsed.

"What mess? What are you talking about?" I croaked as I craned my neck to see the object of Dan's concern.

"This is disgusting!" Dan recoiled at the sight of the dirtied linens and quickly made his way to the shower, with his hands holding his head still aching from his own virus. He swallowed some aspirin and turned on the water.

Finally it dawned on me as I lay there, drained, uncomfortable, emaciated. In spite of my repeated trips to the bathroom in the night, the diarrhea had continued through my sleep. No wonder Dan found it so revolting! I tried to remove myself from the pool of liquefied excrement, but to no avail. I was immobilized by the dehydration. Every movement sent severe pain shooting through my body. My shriveled hands and feet retracted involuntarily in spasms of cramping. I couldn't contain myself any longer and at last, wracked with pain, I shrieked out loud.

Through the tumbling torrents Dan heard me and opened the shower door to ask what was wrong. No answer. He threw a towel around his soaked, soapy body and came into the bedroom. There I lay, skin and bones in my own defecation, writhing with what was obviously excruciating pain. I was a pathetic sight indeed—something one might expect to see in a refugee camp where death and disease ran rampant. The effect on Dan was evident.

"What's wrong? What's the matter, Cherry?" he asked

worriedly. But I could not reply intelligently, I could only groan.

After several minutes I was able to communicate to Dan both the location and the severity of my pain. He tried massaging my back and rubbing my withered extremities but nothing helped. We were so engrossed in my physical trauma, that we almost missed the telephone ringing on the dresser by the bed.

"Hello," Dan impatiently spoke into the receiver. It was my mother. "Yes, Shirley! Maybe you can help us. Cherry's developed a horrible case of the flu overnight and she's in terrible pain. Nothing I'm doing is giving her relief. She's miserable. Do you know any doctors we could call on an emergency basis?"

Following a quick exchange of information, Dan handed me the receiver. I whispered into the phone with a thin, hollow voice answering questions about my mysterious condition. Mommy assured us she would contact a doctor and check back with us. After a quarter of an hour, the phone rang again. This time it was a doctor, one with whom I was completely unfamiliar. He interrogated me regarding my symptoms and concluded that I had suffered a massive loss of potassium as a result of the diarrhea, which produced the pain and severe cramping. He suggested immediate and frequent ingestion of small quantities of orange juice and, if my virally invaded stomach would tolerate it, a banana or two.

We followed the doctor's advice and towards the end of the day I felt much better. Dan, still under the weather himself, had been saddled with most of the cleanup necessitated by my dreadful "accident." I was mortified by my lack of control. Watching him change the linens and scrub the mattress was even more of a humiliation, but I barely had enough strength to sit up. I had no choice but to let him do the job. Or did I?

Only I knew the real reason for the sudden onset of my symptoms and their inexplicable severity. True, I had no idea how extreme the effects of my actions would be but the timing could not have been more opportune. The similarity of my condition to Dan's flu virus had saved me from the painstaking scrutiny of an already suspicious husband. If on any other morning I had unexpectedly awakened to look like "death warmed over," I would certainly have encountered another round of the "third degree." But because of Dan's own illness no one would ever know that on a quick trip to the grocery store the night before, I had impulsively stolen and swallowed sixty laxative tablets.

We spent the following weekend at my parents' house where we could be properly cared for, and I finally stepped on my mother's scale. I was stunned at the dramatic reduction that had occurred. I must have lost fifteen pounds overnight, I thought. I had already put some of the weight back on and yet I was still at least ten pounds below normal! I knew that my weight had dropped, but I had not known how drastically.

In the interim I had cautiously guarded my intake, keeping it as calorically lean as possible until I could assess the effects of my most recent escapade. Dan had long since discarded our own floor scale, claiming it was inaccurate. I had angrily maintained he was just trying to keep me from obsessively guiding my life by the numbers, reading them daily like an astrological forecast. I knew my parents' scale was accurate and I was pleased with its reading. Now I must find a way to keep it from changing.

Fortuitously, Dan's flu lingered on and signs of recovery would give way to relapses. The stress of his job and of coping with my condition lowered his resistance considerably. Once again I took advantage of Dan's virus to claim that my stomach was still incapable of coping with normal food. I introduced a double standard of eating, particularly obvious at dinnertime. A typical scene included a hot plate full of steaming boiled potatoes dripping with butter, two ears of corn on the cob, a juicy hamburger steak, and a side dish of salad served to Dan while I busied myself with a small bowl of cooked cabbage, sprinkled liberally with a seasoned salt substitute.

As Dan's health returned, his patience grew thin and eventually the confrontations over my diet resumed. I had come to enjoy this new thinner body and I resisted putting the quickly lost pounds back on. I knew I could not continue to use the flu excuse unchallenged—unless I, like Dan, was to suffer a series of relapses. I planned them with great care. I stole another large box of laxatives and immediately downed them, this time fully cognizant of, even anticipating, the results. Once again I suffered the diarrhea, a low-grade fever, nausea, dehydration, cramping, sunken eyes, and hollowed cheeks. Once again Dan awoke to find a cadaverous shadow of a wife beside him.

I moved into my old bedroom at my parents' home where I could be watched and attended to while Dan was at work. My recuperation was frustratingly slow and I had everyone worried. The "relapse" had been worse than the initial onset of the "virus" and again I was well below the 100-pound mark.

Attempts to restore me to health entailed an array of remedies. My mother administered daily shots of B-12 in hopes of fortifying my body against the persistent virus. Our church elders visited to anoint me with oil and pray for my healing. We even saw a health expert on a local talk show and decided to have him design a program including vitamins and a special diet high in protein. With practically nothing but dairy products, animal protein, and a powdered supplement as my regular fare, it is no wonder that a subsequent blood test revealed a frighteningly high level of serum cholesterol, along with the usual deficiencies of sodium and potassium.

Meanwhile Dan was forced to tackle the household responsibilities at our apartment on top of his already mountainous work load at the office. Since I was incapacitated, he had no other choice. I didn't think about it much—I tried not to. But I was relieved to be free of the chores. I had begun to find them overwhelmingly burdensome. So I kept myself occupied through the day by shifting my attention between numerous mini-meals and endless crossword puzzles. The couple hired to work for my parents were available to meet any needs or demands I might have. I didn't know then that they were regularly ridiculing Mommy and Daddy behind their backs for letting their daughter starve to death in their own home, when it was really my own doing. I was too absorbed in my cloistered, bizarre existence. I was living like an agoraphobic, barely venturing beyond the confines of my bedroom. When I did make a rare appearance to join the rest of the family for dinner I would bitterly protest against so much as an extra cracker on my plate or the presence of any noodles or rice in my nightly bowl of "chicken soup with meat only."

At this time the Pat Boone family was scheduled to travel to Scandinavia for a concert tour in several countries. Lindy had just given birth to her first child and I was obviously in no condition to sing or dance, so the two older Boone girls stayed home while the rest of the family fulfilled the concert. The guilt I felt for not living up to my professional commitments was only assuaged by the fact that my newborn nephew, Ryan, still required his mother's presence on a full-time basis. With two of us missing I would not have to shoulder full blame for the family's fragmentation.

After more than eight weeks in my parents' Beverly Hills home, Dan finally succeeded in persuading me to return to our own apartment. Even though my weight was still tentatively hovering around 100 pounds I had regained enough strength to be at home alone during the day. He had stopped coming to spend the night at my parents' house several weeks before and he eventually confronted me with our new nonmarriage lifestyle. He was tired of being alone, tired of me still living with my family, tired of my sickness, tired of my pale, emaciated appearance—tired of it all.

The time had come for him to seize control of the situation and if I was going to be his wife, a few things would have to change. If we were going to have a Christian marriage he was going to be the head of our house and I was to be a submissive wife. He would tell me what, when, and how much to eat. It would be up to me to follow through with the instructions. He would tell me what to weigh and when I should reach my goal. Basically, his wish was to be my command, and because this interpretation of biblical passages was an unquestioned tenet of our then Protestant Evangelical faith, I felt morally and spiritually obligated to comply, or at least to try.

As an extra motivation to reach Dan's newly established minimum weight, he promised that if I tipped the scale at 105 pounds before February 20 I could accompany him on a third tour to the Holy Land. I desperately wanted to go but I was only 97 pounds. An eight-pound gain within a mere two-week span seemed an insurmountable task. Part of me wanted nothing more than to obey my husband, to please

God, to gain the weight, and to go with Dan on the ten-day tour. But another persistent part would not permit me to gain a single ounce. I was caught in a struggle between my rational conscious mind and my irrational subconscious. They were playing a game of chess and had reached a stalemate while I looked on helplessly, a powerless pawn.

In one last effort to achieve my 105-pound goal in time to join the tour group, we made an appointment with a nutritionist who specialized in personally designed programs consisting of the rotation of various foods in the diet and based on careful analysis of blood, hair, and urine. It would take several days for the results of the tests to come in so I plunged into volunteer work at Dan's office in preparation for the upcoming tour in order to keep my mind busy while we awaited news from this nutritional guru.

The day before Dan was scheduled to depart, we went to the nutritionist's office. I walked through the door feeling a mixture of hope and fear. When we finally sat down to hear the diagnosis, I had to come to terms with the grim realities of what I had dreaded for weeks.

Not only did he tell us that he thought it would be unwise to travel for health reasons, but he expressed his opinion that mine was a classic case of anorexia nervosa. I had been denying to everyone that anorexia was still a problem. I had even spoken on television about my narrow escape from the horrid disorder. Now this self-proclaimed miracle worker was dashing my claims to smithereens. How dare he? He couldn't have had any idea how completely he had ruined my plans, or the image I had erected to convince people I was free from the clutches of anorexia nervosa. He confirmed to Dan his wildest suspicions. But while he demolished my frail facade, he gave no specific directives for dealing with the malady. Instead, he put me on his rotation diet and one-eighth grain of thyroid. And I put Dan on an airplane. My tears at the terminal were caused not so much by his going as by my staying. Once again I failed everyone.

I spent the next three weeks with Mommy and Debby in Beverly Hills. Now that everyone else was away the house seemed to echo the emptiness I felt inside. My depression grew heavier with each passing day and neither of my authoritarian weight watchers was there to prevent me from moving further down the road to self-destruction. Daddy had always been a strict disciplinarian, tightening the reins of control at the slightest hint of rebellion. In recent months Dan had developed the same approach as an emergency measure since my dangerously low weight was becoming a more and more critical issue. By assuming the role of commander, Dan established what he now admits was a highly inappropriate effort to get things under control. To me it was like a black-and-white movie of my life run in reverse: a replay of scenes of parental discipline and controls. Dan had unknowingly revived an old script that inspired me to play the role of a rebellious child. But even though I resented both my father and my husband, subconsciously I relied on them to protect me from myself.

During this period Mommy stayed home to care for me, although I suspected she also wanted a reason not to have to go on the tour with Daddy, Laury, and Dan. She had always been less overt in her control than Daddy or Dan. Her authority was administered with subtle diplomacy. I think it may have stemmed from her own personal fear of failure to be the perfect mother. It was more of an emotional reflex than a conscious act on her part. Throughout my protracted illness Mommy had usually taken the loving, supportive, even protective approach in her dealings with me.

Somehow, in spite of her selfless giving, I felt as though there were strings attached. If she could give 100 percent maybe it would save me from this horrible nightmare—I would escape, shining once again as a fine specimen of a daughter, simultaneously validating her worth as a mother. But even Mommy had her limits.

Once, she actually followed me into the bathroom and watched me throw up. Her protests were so loud that Debby ran in to see what was happening.

"Cherry, don't do it! You don't have to do it! Fight it! Cherry, stop!" Her pleading and even physical attempts to restrain me proved fruitless.

"I can't help it," I moaned, in determined opposition. "I have to!" Half-crazed, I made my way to the bathroom and forced a vomit. I no longer had to jam fingers down my throat. I had developed a technique of pressing on my stomach which produced the same effect.

When it was all over Debby had to console us both. Mommy was angry, fearful, and crying, while I collapsed into my sister's arms trembling like a frightened mouse. For the first time I felt that I was on the edge of insanity.

When Dan came back from his trip he was near exhaustion. I weighed ninety pounds. In the time it had taken him to lead 1,100 people on a tour of the Holy Land, my body weight had decreased by 10 percent! In desperation, Dan sought the counsel of our family physician, Dr. Newman, who suggested a battery of tests. If nothing conclusive emerged, he recommended immediate hospitalization.

The mere thought of confinement to a hospital bed created panic in the very core of my being. I identified with Job, who said, "My only food is sighs and my groans pour out like water. Whatever I fear comes true, whatever I dread befalls me. For me there is no calm, no peace; my torments banish rest" (Job 3:24–26). Certainly that which I feared was finally coming upon me.

Why? Why should I yield to others I neither knew nor trusted and give up control in the one area of my life that had been mine and mine alone? It was my identity, my realm of expertise, the one thing I could do so well, so much better than anyone else.

In Dr. Newman's office the test results were discussed. EKG, normal. Chest X-ray, fine. Physical exam, good. Urinalysis, okay. Upper GI series, no problem. There appeared to be no cause for what we had been labeling "chronic viremia." Of course, there were the obvious results of my illness: hormone and electrolyte imbalance, tired blood, a starved body that was consuming itself for lack of nutrition. My digestive system had suffered such repeated abuse that the intestines had collapsed. My menstrual cycle had once again ceased. As a defense against starvation, my inessential biological systems had shut down to conserve energy and sustain life.

Now the verdict was in and the gavel sounded with a heavy crack. The sentence was passed: hospitalization. Imprisonment! Two weeks of solitary confinement were ordered for intensive examination. I had no freedom, no choice, no self-determination—no me, I thought bitterly.

The following day I signed my rights away at the admissions desk of Century City Hospital. I wasn't even permitted to walk to my room. I was forced into a wheelchair and pushed like a baby in a stroller! At least they could have allowed me the dignity of walking on my own— I needed that last bit of calorie-burning exercise.

Hospitalization was humiliating enough but, on top of that, I was assigned three full-time nurses who rotated on eight-hour shifts for twenty-four-hour surveillance. This babysitting angered and embarrassed me. While I got along well with them, their constant presence was a reminder that I was being policed. They were required to report to Dr. Newman anything they observed regarding my condition, so occasionally one of my uniformed sentinels would scribble on a telltale clipboard.

When I checked in on Monday, March 21, 1977, I weighed approximately 80 pounds. Between crossword puzzles, television, and meticulously extending my three mandatory meals to two hours apiece, I kept myself busy enough to avoid lunacy.

I was provided with my own menus and if my request couldn't be met by the kitchen, an effort was made to satisfy my desires. The primary goal was to get me to eat. If trips to the health-food store were requested ten times a day to ensure that I ate, then it would be done. Frozen yogurt, carob-chip cookies—whatever I wanted would magically appear as if I were Aladdin commanding the genie in his lamp. When the goodies arrived I would savor them slowly.

In spite of all the security I managed to persist in my inane behavior. For example, meal breaks were required for my nurses. When they went to the cafeteria for twenty minutes, I took advantage of their absence by vigorously exercising. In the secluded therapy bath I did leg lifts. But the most incredible obstinance of all was my habitual showering or teeth brushing, which strategically followed each meal. With the door closed and water running I proceeded to vomit my carefully prepared meals. I was never apprehended in my games.

Dan came straight from work almost every night to visit me, if only for fifteen minutes. He urged me to view my hospital stay as a rest, even a vacation, and in many ways it was just that. It was a chance to be away from all the people and pressures that persistently beset me at my parents' house and our apartment. I was alone with my problems— there was no one else to complicate things with troublesome emotional reactions.

My conversations with Dan in the hospital were among the most civil and loving in weeks. For me the breathing room was helpful; for Dan the fact that at last something definitive was being done eased his burden of responsibility for a sickly, stubborn wife.

Dan was not my only regular visitor. Almost every night Mommy would stop by briefly to check on me. At some point during my hospitalization every member of the family came by to see how I was doing and to drop off a card or a gift or just have a chat. I was touched by their commitment to me.

Mommy was the most faithful in interrupting her chaotic schedule to drive to the hospital during visiting hours. But it was in an evening session with Mommy that all hell seemed to break loose.

During my first week in the hospital, Dan had engaged in deep soul searching regarding my condition, meeting several times with Dr. Newman, with friends, and with our pastor, Jack Hayford. The general consensus was that Dan and I should consider moving away from Los Angeles; that I needed to sever the strong cords binding me to my parents (especially Mommy), and that we should seek professional psychiatric help in dealing with my anorexia. Everyone he talked to agreed that these steps had to be taken for the good of all.

At the prompting of a Seattle relative Dan phoned psychiatrist Raymond Vath, who had successfully treated many cases of depression, family problems, and even anorexia nervosa. Dr. Vath also saw the need to remove me from my current surroundings. In spite of a crowded calendar, he was willing to fit me in if we would be willing to make the move to Seattle and commit ourselves to the ongoing therapy that would be required in a case like mine. To Dan it sounded like a long-awaited answer to our prayers.

That night Dan came to the hospital earlier than usual with rekindled hope that a solution to our dilemma might still exist. This new option was certainly one of the only remaining unexplored avenues. Perhaps this was the rainbow after the storm that would lead us to the much-sought-after prizes of health, peace, and joy.

My initial reaction to Dan's proposal was positive. A clean start in a new environment and someone who might have the answers we so desperately needed was an appealing alternative to the doom and futility we felt thus far. Dan, by this time a vice-president in the corporation for which he worked, prepared for his resignation. Meanwhile, his parents assured him that we would be welcome to stay with them indefinitely. Now the only obstacle remaining was my family—a personal and professional challenge.

Suddenly the full consequences of the impending change sunk in and my optimistic smiles gave way to confused tears. How could I leave my family? They were the only friends I had left! And what about performing? We had already begun working on new material for the summer tour! The show would require total rewriting with five members instead of six. And all of the money spent on costumes, musical arrangements, choreography. All of it, I feared, would be utterly wasted because of me.

The choice was obvious but no less painful for all its clarity. To say goodbye to family and to performing would be the hardest things I had ever done. My emotions were fraught with ambivalence. I wanted to be well and I wanted to be the wife Dan desired, needed, and deserved. But I did not want to leave my family—my sisters, my parents, my sweet new nephew—and I didn't want to stop singing, traveling, and performing on stage.

Or did I? No rehearsals, no fittings, no pressure to look and be perfect, to pretend to be something I was not. The thought soothed me. To be able to relax for a while with no responsibilities, no schedules, no plans—it seemed like a sweet dream. And with one word I could cause it to become a reality . . . "YES!" I would go!

An inner sense of freedom filled me immediately, something that had been unknown to me since early childhood. It was exhilarating! An adventure awaited us, just Dan and me! It almost made me giggle to think about it.

When Dan left my room that night he said he would make all of the necessary arrangements and set the wheels in motion for our big move. The next day he would talk to his boss, and explain that he would have to terminate his employment for the sake of my health. I told him I would be praying for him.

He called me the next afternoon to inform me that we had a green light on all fronts. Dr. Vath was working to fit us into his schedule, Dan's parents had a room ready, and, to his amazement, Dan's employer not only agreed that this step was right but wished him well, making no protest regarding Dan's sudden decision to resign. Dan held a key position in the business so we were both pleasantly surprised and encouraged by his generous support. That night, Dan informed my parents of our plans to leave.

"Pat, I believe that if Cherry is to survive, to recover, we must seek expert psychiatric help. I have contacted a doctor in Seattle. It will mean moving from Los Angeles." Dan spoke haltingly to his concerned and surprised father-in-law.

"Don't you think there are doctors down here who could handle this, Dan?" Daddy searched for an alternative.

"We've pretty well concluded that we need to get away. Dr. Newman agrees . . . ."

"What about the recording and television contracts. We may want to think about those . . ."

"Dr. Newman says that in a case of serious illness there are no contracts," Dan replied.

"I understand. But how does Cherry feel about it?"

"She's ready to go. Of course she has deeply mixed feelings—but she is willing to take the plunge."

The conversation was brief and decisive. Dan, fearing much stiffer resistance, heaved a deep sigh of relief.

The following day Mommy came to visit. We discussed the meeting that had taken place the previous night. Although she had avoided being present at the time, Daddy reported our plans to her.

"Honey, what do *you* want to do? Do you want to stop performing with the family?" she probed.

"No, Mommy, I don't want to stop singing with you. I love doing it! And I don't want to break up the act! But if Dan is willing to quit his job and sacrifice everything for me, it's the least I can do. It's my fault he's having to do all of this in the first place!" My eyes brimmed with tears and my voice cracked as I tried to suppress the lump rising in my throat.

"Well, if you're going to stop performing with us, I'll just quit too. I've never really enjoyed it like you girls have, and the pressure is . . ."

"No! No! Mommy, don't! If you quit the whole thing will

fall apart and it will be my fault! I feel so bad already. Please, please, don't quit the show!"

Fear and guilt overtook me and I began to heave heavy sobs. Realizing the effect I was having on so many lives was too much to bear. Mommy tried to convince me that she would not leave the stage, but I knew that for years she had been uncomfortable with her role as entertainer. She had even talked about quitting before now. I was afraid that, if she did quit now, once again I would be her scapegoat—her excuse. If I were the first domino to fall, causing all the rest to tumble, I could never forgive myself. But we were beyond the point of return.

I checked out of the hospital on Saturday, April 2, a few pounds heavier but not really any healthier. Eager anticipation, however, was swelling inside. The fresh spring air seemed to be full of life and hope. I felt like a caterpillar emerging from its cocoon to challenge the world as a new creation. The unknown struggles that lay ahead simulated that "emerging" process. But there were to be difficult times when I would fear the cocoon had changed from womb to tomb.

Still extremely underweight, I was not permitted to help Dan pack. Over the next three weeks he boxed everything himself. We tied up loose ends, saw our close friends one last time, and prepared to begin our journey up the coast. Fearing the unknown, dreading goodbyes, and feeling the burden of responsibility for this radical change, I lost even more precious pounds.

One day just prior to leaving, I noticed my wedding ring was missing! I had gotten so thin it had fallen off my finger unnoticed. I was horrified! The sentimental value far outweighed its monetary value, and now it was gone forever! How could I have been so negligent?

Dan's attempts to comfort me were not completely successful but he did point out the symbolic timing of my loss. I was embarking on a new life with my husband, away from my parents. Maybe, for some reason, God had allowed me to lose the old ring so that at some point in the future we could replace the old with the new, just as we were hoping to replace our past despair with new fulfillment.

Finally our departure day arrived. My parents reconciled themselves to my absence from home and the family show. They even gave me their blessings to embark on this new journey.

On April 26, with tearful goodbyes behind us, Dan mounted his big, touring motorcycle and I climbed behind the wheel of our car. Dan wondered if I could really go the distance—he said my arms were "thin as noodles." I was determined to hold up my end of our trek northward towards the health, hope, and light we believed were awaiting us at the end of this awful tunnel. In spite of our optimism, a kind of "last chance" quality permeated the air.

My fork danced lightly across the top of a slice of Melba O'Neill's renowned blackberry pie. I pushed tiny flakes of crust around on my plate. Dan and I sat with his parents in their bedroom. For two weeks we had been sharing the waterfront Shelton house with Dan's parents, Bill and Melba, his twelve-year-old sister, Katie, and his brother, Steve, and his wife, Debbie. Until now the issue of my anorexia had been studiously avoided. Finally the time was right to talk.

In the few days we had been there I managed to make

things awkward for everyone. When Dan's parents agreed to open their house to us they had no idea that the presence of a person with anorexia nervosa is one of the most disruptive forces a family can face. An anoretic is very similar to an alcoholic—once the habit takes over, free choice gives way to overpowering bondage, victimizing the family and friends of the sick individual. The sufferer repeatedly resolves to "take the cure," only to fall "off the wagon" in a moment of weakness. They end up deceiving, manipulating, and hurting the very people they love most as they perpetuate their self-destructive pursuits.

This similarity was one of the topics of discussion as we met in the bedroom that night. There had been tension in the air due to a lack of knowledge about anorexia and to my typically bizarre behavior. Almost immediately after my arrival, I made complaints about the O'Neill family's eating habits. Even before developing my obsessions with food and thinness, the meals I had eaten with my family almost never included bread, potatoes, french fries, pasta, fried foods, creamy casseroles, or even red meat. I was raised on salads, seafood, poultry, wild rice, and fresh vegetables neither sauced nor buttered. We rarely had gravy, and pork was unheard of. A lamb chop, steak, or veal dish appeared from time to time and even a pot of my mom's chili simmered on the stove once or twice a year. But hamburgers, potatoes, Jell-O salad, and rich sweets were completely foreign to my family's daily fare.

Suddenly I was faced with not only *having* to eat, but having to eat things I did not want or like. I wasn't about to fill my bowl with sugar-coated cereal in the morning, and forget the french fries, bread, and Jell-O! If I was going to gain weight it wouldn't be with what I considered junk.

So I put saccharin in my watered-down hot cereal, in my homemade special dressing, and in my beverages. I used salt substitute on anything for which the rest of the O'Neills used regular salt or butter. When Dan ruled out my continued use of "fake" sugar and salt, he unwittingly put his parents in the position of having to hide my precious calorie-free chemicals from me. Battle lines were being drawn in the kitchen.

I knew if I could just appear to be ingesting large quantities of food while keeping the calorie count low I could trick everyone into thinking I was trying to gain weight. But now that Dan had educated himself on the caloric values of cabbage, cantaloupe, and cottage cheese, my only recourse was to limit the portions of my mandatory three meals a day.

Dan's mom, unaware of the unending frustration he had been enduring throughout our marriage, still felt that he was, on occasion, unduly harsh with me. On one such occasion Dan's now easily sparked anger spilled over at her. "Butt out, Mom!" I remember him warning her as she tried to protect me from his scolding. Dan's temper may have surprised her; there was no way she could have known what I had put him through in preceding months.

Her good nature and kind-hearted approach were evident one morning when we greeted each other in the kitchen. "My, my, dear," she said as she gave my slightly less than gaunt face a friendly pat. "You look like you're feeling better this morning!" That was what she said. What I heard was, "Your face certainly is filling out!" For the next two months I made sure that my face resembled a shrunken head. What she intended as an encouraging compliment I took as a crushing insult. At the first opportunity, I stole a box of laxatives to ensure that I wouldn't look like I was "feeling better."

In fact, it was a batch of stolen pills that had finally precipitated our family summit conference. Dan confronted me upon my return from a trip to the grocery store, demanding to search both the shopping bags and my purse for contraband. I had been weighing in mysteriously low and he knew I was back to my old tricks. His investigation produced a handful of little white laxatives hidden in my wallet. He marched me into our bedroom and proceeded to fly into a tirade, blasting away with questions, blistering accusations, and criticisms. Knowing that his unassuming mother must be hearing the fiasco through the thin bedroom door was humiliating enough, but I was utterly mortified when Dan ordered me to strip as proof that I was not hiding anything beneath my clothes. Embarrassed and tearful I still maintained that I was not keeping anything more from Dan. He was not satisfied and continued to ask about laxatives, shoplifting, and saccharin. He had developed highly effective interrogation techniques full of psychological and semantic entrapments. Finally my resistance shattered and the truth poured out. Yes, I had been taking laxatives regularly; yes, they had been stolen; and yes, I had stashed some saccharin tablets in a secret place.

When the horrid scene ended I was huddled in a pathetic heap on the floor wailing like a wounded animal, pleading for forgiveness, and crying out for God's help. Dan realized it was time to call a family meeting that same night.

As we congregated around the bed, my eyes were riveted on the floor. I sat down and drew my knees up for extra warmth—I was always cold and the dampness of Washington's annual spring showers intensified the feeling. But my low body temperature was no match for the icy emptiness I felt inside.

As we explained the dynamics of my disorder my tears flowed freely. I felt sorrow, shame, remorse, and asked my parents-in-law please to forgive me. Eager as they were to comfort me with their forgiveness, they were still unsure as to why it was even necessary. For what was I seeking their forgiveness?

I expressed my deep desire to put an end to my games and to move on with my life. But still a persistent inability to see myself realistically compelled me into self-abusive behavior.

"Sometimes I can really see myself like I am," I declared with a combination of pride and discomfiture. Dan's mother could not comprehend such a statement. It was indeed one of the more baffling aspects of my illness—I had lost all perspective of reality. My brain was starved, my body image distorted. To others this was a fascinating, even frightening curiosity; for me, it was a grave, destructive maladaptation. The entire problem with its far-reaching ramifications and terrifying potentialities seemed to paralyze me. Total health was my ultimate goal but it eluded me at every turn.

Towards the end of our conference, Dan's father suggested a simple yet profound concept—a new approach to fighting this menacing foe.

"Well, it seems to me," he said calmly, "that instead of trying to handle the whole problem all at once, you should just take each day as a new beginning, a clean slate. Just concentrate on one day at a time. Don't dwell on yesterday or worry about tomorrow. Focus on today and move step by step, and when today is over, evaluate it, set it aside, and face the next day the same way. That would probably be a lot easier on everyone—especially you, Cherry.''

What a freeing thought! My perfectionist point of view prohibited me from realizing that improvement could be made effectively in increments. To my mind, it had always been all or nothing. My issues were black and white—there was no room for gray. Now a whole new realm of possibilities had opened up for me. Clearly, the mountain still had to be moved—there was no getting around it. But it could be moved truckload by truckload, or even, if necessary, tablespoon by tablespoon! If a thimble were all I could carry, then, with God's help, I would move that monstrosity one thimbleful at a time! From this time on, the loving acceptance and unshakeable support of Dan's family, particularly his parents, became a major force in my growth towards the goal of health.

But the pivotal factor in this new growth was introduced on Wednesday, May 18, 1977, when Dan and I rode the elevator to the nineteenth floor of Seattle's Cabrini Medical Tower. My heart sank into my stomach with the stark realization that I was going to my first appointment with a psychiatrist. Why me? My sisters had been raised by the same parents in the same environment. Why was *I* the one requiring psychiatric help? It seemed so unjust! Life was playing some practical joke and I was the brunt of it—or, worse yet, the punch line.

As I was experiencing pangs of guilt, Dan was breathing much easier. We were finally going to take affirmative action to conquer this thing. We were about to meet the wonder-working Dr. Vath—the specialist with all of the answers, or so we hoped. Dan expected to drop me off at the doctor's office saying, "Okay, *fix* her!" and then return to pick me up later. Instead he got something entirely different, something he had not bargained for in his early telephone arrangements with Dr. Vath. Dan's role was not to be merely that of a chauffeur for a neurotic wife. Beginning with that first appointment, Dan and I were together for every session. His involvement in my psychotherapy would be total.

CHAPTER EIGHT

High-Wire Act

Wednesday, May 18. Cherry eighty-eight pounds. Drove to Seattle, Dr. Vath appointment. He is a graying, friendly looking man in his mid-forties, and very comforting. He is beginning to search out Cherry's world view, background factors, and the input that has led to a long-term self-destructive process. Her ideas of love, relationships, and conditional aspects of both were dicussed. The hour passed quickly and was really quite encouraging.*

My impressions of our opening session with Ray Vath were similar to Dan's, but I recall a sense of frustration that more was not accomplished. I did most of the talking, reviewing the same old story once again. I hoped for something more constructive than the quiet doctor's occasional "uh-huh . . . mmm . . . I see," accompanied by the regular nodding of his bespectacled head.

At least it was a beginning. Our one remaining flicker of hope would have to work—there was nothing else left.

Because the round-trip drive from Shelton to Dr. Vath's Seattle office was four hours, we frequently stayed with close friends, Dan and Chrissie Ganfield, who had a two-

* The italicized excerpts in this chapter are taken from Dan's journal entries for 1977.

bedroom apartment in a lovely area called Greenlake. We spent four days following our first therapy session in stimulating conversation continuing into the wee hours. The Ganfields, longtime friends of Dan, accepted me with open arms and loving hearts and into their deeply rooted friendship with Dan. They were aware of my illness but were not knowledgeable on the subject of anorexia nervosa. Nonetheless they responded to me with the understanding and warmth I so desperately wanted and needed.

Between our first and second appointments with Dr. Vath, some important things happened. I confessed to Dan my continuation of covert anoretic tricks since the preceding October. For eight months I had lied, stolen, gorged, vomited, abused laxatives, and had succeeded in deceiving doctors, nurses, parents, friends . . . everyone, including him. The examinations, the tests, the hospital stay, and the private nurses had all been an enormous waste. I hadn't had the flu, I admitted, or chronic viremia. I had caused it all myself. I alone was responsible for the huge medical bills, hours of lab work, and months of concern on the part of my husband and family. I told the whole truth.

Dan was stunned by the revelation. I knew he might never trust me again. But strangely, in spite of the attending trauma, I felt relief at dumping the burden.

Then came an unexpected phone call from Dan's second cousin Darlene Cunningham. She is married to Loren Cunningham, the founder of Youth with a Mission, the organization Dan worked with overseas. Their international headquarters was located in Kailua-Kona, Hawaii. As a member of the family she had been apprised of my condition and felt that a restful time in their Kona community could be therapeutic. Although we could not accept the invitation immediately, we regarded it with interest as a future possibility.

Friday, May 27. For the second time Cherry and I drove to Seattle for an appointment with Dr. Vath. Later to the Ganfields' apartment. We had another interesting and, I believe, therapeutic session with Dr. Vath. Topics discussed: Cherry's worth or value (absolute and relative), admissions of anoretic activity, incremental recovery ideas, my attempts to control Cherry's behavior, Cherry's ambivalence about being controlled. More discussion with each other and the Ganfields. I am attempting to give her more room, knowing that there is more risk, but believing there will be more of God's grace.

"Well, tell me, Dan. Do you really believe that you can control Cherry's behavior in an absolute sense?" Dr. Vath asked intently from his padded, leather armchair. Dan and I, together on the sofa across the room, sat in silence as he contemplated his answer to the doctor's question. After considerable thought, Dan replied.

"Yes, I could handcuff her, tie her to a chair, and force-feed her. Yeah, I could control her if I had to, but I see your point. Eventually the time would come to set her free and she would do the same thing to herself all over again."

"That's right, Dan. The whole problem of trying to extend absolute control over another member of the human race is that ultimately it's quite impossible. Do you see? It's frustrating to the controller and to the one being controlled and I'm convinced, Dan, it is an exercise in futility if, in fact, the controlled individual does not choose to cooperate. And Cherry is a good example of the person who is looking for the security of external control while striving to be independent from the very control she thinks she needs. Is that right, Cherry?"

He seemed to understand exactly how I felt—somehow he was feeling it with me. His compassion freed me to vent emotions regarding control and the confusing role it played in my life.

Together we determined that because I deeply desired to please my parents and, now, Dan, and because I never trusted myself to measure up to their expectations, I allowed them and even unconsciously encouraged them to set boundaries for me. Fear of failure overshadowed my desire for self-determination but now a struggle between the submissive Cherry and the emerging, independent Cherry intensified. The areas of weight control and eating behavior were the battlefield on which it was being waged.

Perhaps it was an attention-getting device—if I couldn't hold the spotlight by being the "perfect little girl," I could certainly ensure parental attention by requiring their total control. Whatever the cause, their control continued long beyond the point of propriety and now the maturing process, which should have occurred during adolescence, was in full swing. I was, in effect, making attempts, inappropriate and self-destructive as they might be, to declare my freedom, to grow up. Part of me was still a frightened child whose growth had been stunted by fear, while another part was desiring to take responsibility for my own life which, ironically, was being destroyed as a result of the ongoing, unresolved conflict.

When we left the office that afternoon to meet our friends Dan and Chrissie, I sensed that Dan had reached a profound realization about his attempts to control. Dr. Vath boiled it all down in one succinct and starkly truthful observation: "In the end they will do what they will do and I will do what

I will do." Dan and Dan Ganfield had coined a phrase in earlier years that conveyed the concept equally well: People are free to "choose their own blues." Dan knew at that moment that he must give me that freedom, no matter what I would do with it and regardless of the cost to him or to me. Changes were obviously needed in both of us, but they would not come easily.

Three weeks passed before our third appointment with the doctor and in the meantime things took several interesting turns. Less than a week later Dan discovered I weighed a disappointing eighty-eight pounds. After several days of progress I had taken a major step backwards. Apparently my regression triggered a similar phenomenon in Dan's response. His tendencies to control surfaced again and flare-ups increased as I rebelled against his authoritative approach.

None too soon an opportunity arose for us to house-sit for a family from Vashon Island, a small land mass in the middle of the Puget Sound. It was a chance to be alone together for the first time in six months. We needed a rest, some relaxation, and privacy. When I look back on those seven days I see them as the happiest and most hopeful I'd experienced in years.

Dan and I were the only ones in the waterfront house that sat at the end of a long private driveway. The setting was quiet and secluded. The peaceful environment seemed to whisper permission to eat, enjoy, and be myself. I took great pleasure in both preparing and consuming substantial meals that consisted of my favorite, and usually high-calorie, foods.

I was able to loosen the chains of my bondage and accept the weight I was gaining without feeling threatened or fearful. Dan and I were free to unwind, discuss our mutual problems, and thoroughly relax. One morning as we slept in, I actually woke myself up laughing at a humorous dream. I could not recall ever experiencing such boundless glee on a subconscious level. I took it as a powerfully positive sign.

When we returned to Shelton, I weighed 101 pounds. In just twelve days I had gained thirteen pounds, most of which had been added during our little one-week vacation! Dan was thrilled, but I was surprised and a bit fearful. The drastic change took me off guard and although I gave mental assent to it, fear rose inside. I was walking a tightrope between my old familiar behavior, which would certainly lead to death, and the new unknown path that promised life. It was a dangerous time. I was attempting to smash through a monumental barrier. The hurdle towards health was about to be negotiated. Thankfully, our third session with Dr. Vath was just around the corner.

Friday, June 17. Our session with Dr. Vath was somewhat one-sided as Cherry did most of the talking. Therapy was administered, I believe, as "secret" information was shared. Again, childhood history became an important factor. Discipline, overcontrol, facades, family secrets, and problems from earlier generations were topics of conversation. . . .

With only two hours of therapy behind us, Dr. Vath had shown himself to be an empathetic and trustworthy friend. I found myself sharing some very personal family secrets with someone I had known only for a month.

Hesitant at first to divulge some of the darker facts for fear of ruining reputations, I tested the water by telling tales that involved only my immediate family. When I felt it safe and concluded that images were not worth protecting if they camouflaged reality, I freely related stories about extended-family faux pas that pertained to the development of my illness. I began to comprehend, through my own narration, some of the reasons for my parents' behavior and why their parents had done what they had done. Discussion of familial traits and tendencies created new areas of self-awareness and while I did not feel excused from my own responsibility for my illness, it did allow me to lighten my burden by sharing it with the generations that had gone before me. I was able to give up some of my guilt.

The following Sunday we met Loren and Darlene as they passed through Seattle from Hawaii. They renewed their invitation to Kona for a time of "mending." Our drive back to Shelton was alive with excitement as we considered the possibility.

Three days later Dan and I drove back to Seattle—this time to meet my father at the airport. He was only making a brief stop to spend the evening with Dan and me on the way to some professional appearances but we had arranged to have dinner together between his connecting flights.

A significant factor that emerged in the course of our meeting was that plans for my future performances with the family were still being formulated. Of course, nothing would be forced. They were only ideas, Daddy reassured. Still, I observed that Dan was waxing wary of the old "family fingers" and their unconscious way of wrangling me back into the fold. His response to Daddy's friendly feelers regarding my participation was understandably guarded. The delicate healing process had only just begun and even Daddy had displayed unrestrained elation over my obvious weight gain. Dan wanted to guarantee its continuation without interruptions or setbacks. By strengthening the family ties at this strategic juncture we could thwart my long-overdue growth towards independence.

I think Daddy understood our concerns. As we shuttled him to his flight we were grateful that no pressure was applied and that Daddy's greatest desire was my health and well-being.

Friday, June 24. I felt quite good about our session with Dr. Vath. We discussed our upcoming visit to L.A. for Cherry's birthday, Hollywood's "plastic" values and peer pressure, life scripting (behavior patterns which we absorb from parents and environment). Dr. Vath is pleased overall with Cherry's progress. There was more of a spiritual "tilt" to Vath's comments this session. I am finding myself trying to "psyche him out" a bit.

My anxiety about returning to the old haunts of Hollywood must have been apparent. Even Dan had to admit to a certain degree of apprehension as he thought about me trying to face the challenges of plunging into the same environment which had been the crucible for my craziness. Although intellectually I acknowledged the superficial values and the shallow view that one's appearance is all-important, I was unable to alleviate my fears. Why was I so afraid to go home?

"Well, like Shakespeare said, 'all the world's a stage,' and people are only actors. It seems that each one of us is handed a script by our parents which we tend to live out whether we are aware of it or not." I wasn't sure where he was leading with his observation but I listened to Dr. Vath with interest.

"What I think I hear you saying, Cherry, is that you've changed the scenery; you've moved on to the second act, so to speak, and you're afraid that by going back to Los Angeles and the old setting from the first act, you might fall into your old role. Being surrounded by the same old scenery and acting with the same old characters might cause you to read the same old lines since that's all you've known to do in that environment. Is that right?"

Once again he interpreted my deepest fears with the utmost of clarity. He went on to explain the phenomenon of "scripting" as developed by Eric Berne, M.D., in his book, *What Do You Say After You Say Hello?* With uncanny consistency, people tend to repeat the same basic plot lived out by their parents. For some it can be a positive experience, but most of us are aware of some things in the lives of our parents we would just as soon avoid. Unfortunately, few of us are conscious of this scripting process and even fewer know how to rewrite it creatively. As Dr. Vath said, modeling by parents or others within our particular sphere of influence is our most powerful behavioral determinant.

Eating habits are a reflection of family rituals ingrained from infancy. The foods we eat, when we eat them, the way we eat, and the amount we eat are frequently the direct result of early and often unconscious training. Even our attempts to alter our eating patterns can be seen as reactions stemming from the same root. For example, eating less can be a fear reaction to becoming like obese parents while eating more may be an attempt to compensate for a deprived childhood. As I faced my Beverly Hills homecoming I felt myself regressing towards a relapse unless I could establish my eating practices on a new basis.

"Well, the design features of the human body are quite ingenious, Cherry, and the Master Designer built in a little-known but very effective device in the brain called an appestat. It is a mechanism that lets us know when our body has had enough food—in essence it tells us when we are full. But it whispers; it doesn't impose itself on our will. We need to educate ourselves to listen to the appestat instead of ignoring it and living by the scripts we've been given. Your script may tell you to eat or not to eat for any number of inappropriate reasons, but unless there is some overriding biological problem, your appestat will never lie. If we discover what, when, why, and how much is right for *your* body and for *your* health, we can replace the old script with a new one. Does that sound reasonable . . . hm?"

It did. But how would I do it? And why had I developed an eating disorder in the first place? Obviously there had been unfulfilled emotional needs in my life. The need for acceptance and approval—the need to be perfect—had been a driving force that ultimately brought me to the brink of death. In my early years I equated my worth as a person with the level of my performance and I felt that the love and approval of other people would be conditional upon my perfection. Therefore, I expended every effort to be the best I could possibly be in any given area of endeavor, only to repeatedly fall short of my goals and risk losing value in the eyes of others. Trying even harder, only to miss the mark again and again, resulted in compounded guilt and self-hatred.

"Perfectionism is a terribly frustrating approach to living. There is always room to improve so you never reach the point of absolute perfection. And practice has never made perfect—practice makes better. Does that make sense, Cherry?" Dr. Vath asked. It did.

"It sounds to me like you don't like yourself very much and you've told me the reason is guilt for failing to measure up to the expectations of people you love and want to love you. After all, Jesus said that we're supposed to love our neighbors *more* than ourselves—isn't that right?"

I looked at the doctor quizzically. That wasn't right! Jesus had said to love our neighbor *as* ourselves. Suddenly I realized what Dr. Vath was trying to do. He was teaching me to think—to discover on my own the fallacy of my most basic presuppositions. As my eyes widened with the dawning of new truth, I saw a wise grin sweep across his face.

"No, that's not right, is it. He said to love your neighbor *as* yourself. I'm convinced that unless we learn to love ourselves we can never really appropriately love others. Now all we have to do is help you to learn to love *you* a little bit. Does that sound like a good idea?"

It sounded like a wonderful idea. But how could I learn to love someone I had come to loathe so intensely?

"You've been judging yourself harshly based on your inability to measure up to your standards of perfection. We need to help you find another yardstick with which to determine your worth and value as a person. I'm certain that we can find some very positive things about yourself— things you can learn to love. Don't you think so?"

I sheepishly nodded as I stared at my lap. "I guess so. But I can't imagine it. It seems like I've hated myself for so long that I don't know how else to feel. The thought of learning a whole new way to live scares me."

"I know. It is frightening," Dr. Vath concurred. "But it's pretty easy to let go of a nickle when someone is handing you a one-hundred-dollar bill, don't you think?"

With a new sense of confidence, I boarded a jet bound for Los Angeles the day before my twenty-third birthday. Although there were occasional lapses into unfounded fears of fatness or rejection based on my changed appearance and emerging independent identity, the trip itself was free of any major incidents. A birthday party arranged by my mother, which included friends and family members, produced some weight-conscious anxiety, but with the endless comments I received on my "new beauty," I actually permitted myself to begin believing that everyone was genuinely pleased with me. I resisted old temptations to secretly question their underlying motives.

While we were there I managed to do two rather special things: make a record with my sisters and buy a new wedding ring with the $777 Dan had given me for my birthday (my birthday that year was on 7/7/77). A new ring, a new year of life, a new phase of relationship with Dan—I was high with optimism!

Tuesday, July 19. The life-script concept (Eric Berne) is an extremely interesting idea and presents the possibility of a "creative rewrite." This offers a real hope. The healing process is a reality now, accelerating with continued realization and understanding.

On the next drive from Shelton into Seattle, Dan and I listened to a tape of Dr. Vath teaching a counseling seminar about scripting. Hearing the tapes between sessions with the doctor was like getting extra doses of his psychotherapeutic medicine. Even Dan was grateful for the extra input as he began to realize the many ways in which I was the product of influences in my past that had come to weigh heavily on a very fragile, delicate, and complicated child. He admitted, to my amazement, that to some degree I had indeed been programmed by circumstances and environment, but especially by parents and family.

Twelve days after our fifth appointment with Dr. Vath, we

were airborne again—this time for a Boone family reunion in Florida. Daddy's parents organized the event around their forty-fifth wedding anniversary. The idea was a lovely one. Unfortunately it was ruined by a disastrous turn of events.

Perhaps it was wearing a bathing suit all day, or the pressure of everyone knowing about my problem but avoiding discussion of it. Maybe it was having several cans of my grandmother's special butter-fried, salted pecans on hand (*nobody* can eat just one). Or was it the power of the Boone script, which says that eating is a social pastime, each mouthful of Southern hospitality permeated with mother's love? Whatever the cause, the effect was devastating.

Worried about my still shaky control of food intake, I started slightly restricting my diet while we were traveling. My tendency to eat more food later in the day, combined with the uncertainty of meals on the road, necessitated near total abstinence until dinner. Once I had eaten my evening meal I could more carefully gauge the calories of subsequent snacks. I couldn't threaten my delicate balance! Needless to say, my refusal to eat a normal breakfast or lunch seemed a bad sign to Dan.

After celebrating Nana and Papa's anniversary, I excused myself to the restroom while children played on the beach and adults conversed. I had eaten too much—somehow I had lost control and went beyond the point of comfortable fullness. The cake, ice cream, and salted nuts sat on top of dinner like an unwelcome lump in my stomach. There had been a few other occasions like this in recent weeks when I was too full and relieved myself by jamming my finger down my throat. I felt twinges of guilt afterwards but determined not to let it become a habit. I rationalized that

Dan need not know. I told myself that this would be the last time, at least for a while, as I leaned over the toilet seat.

"That's a pretty sight!" a muffled voice filtered through the window. "That's really great! Just go ahead! You ought to be real proud of yourself!"

Shock, fear, and embarrassment jolted me upright and I saw Dan peering at me through the window. Oh God! Oh God! No! Not this! Not this *again!* There was nothing I could do. I was caught in the act! Cherry, you idiot! Why did you let this happen again? Why?

Dan and I tried to disguise our heated emotions as we said early goodnights to the group. On the walk home restraint was abandoned.

"You liar! I suppose you're going to tell me that's the first time you've thrown up!" Dan exploded with rage. I tried to defend myself through my tears.

"I'm sorry, Dan! I'm sorry. Really!"

"Yeah, I'm sure you are—sorry you got caught! What about the other times when you weren't caught? Tell me about those if you're so sorry!"

Ashamed by my lack of honesty and afraid of further wrath I denied my recent vomiting.

"You really are crazy if you think I'm about to swallow that one. Tell the truth!" he insisted.

"Okay! I have thrown up before!"

"When? How many times?"

"I can't remember."

"Has it been that often that you can't remember?"

"I haven't done it that many times—just a few! I promise! I'd have to think about when they were." By now I was crying uncontrollably.

"You looked disgusting in there, you know it? You really

are sick! Happy reunion!" he muttered walking ahead of me to our hotel.

Later that night apologies were exchanged but I knew Dan had been jarred. In spite of ourselves, our spirits sagged to a new low. We flew from Florida to Michigan, where we watched from the grandstands as the "Boone Family" performed on stage at the Ionia County Fair. Objectively, the show was enjoyable, but inside I felt left out and disowned. And it was all my fault!

Thursday, August 11. Dr. Vath appointment. Once again our encounter with Dr. Vath was stimulating and most reassuring. We discussed Cherry's rapid response, turning from family temporarily, establishing identity, and Hawaii. Our relationship with Ray [Dr. Vath] is becoming more of a friendship than a clinical alliance.

Amidst the talk of progress and hope, we couldn't bear to divulge to our doctor the frightful affair in Florida. I responded rapidly with weight gain and I was maintaining a steady 111 pounds. I also experienced a temporary but unexpected hostility towards my parents that manifested itself in my phone conversations with them. It was as if I felt a sort of glee in being as uninformative as possible. Their hands had been in every facet of my life when I was growing up, and now I was enjoying my power to keep them at a distance and in the dark.

I was developing an identity independent of my family and the prospect of Hawaii seemed to be conducive to its continuing emergence. But deep down I was feeling the beginnings of the familiar hidden desperation. Would it all slip through our fingers so close to recovery? I could not bear to disappoint my new friend and professional confessor—I did not want to break the spell he had cast. This attitude was a grave mistake.

Thursday, September 1. Another session with Dr. Vath. I shared my present rather laid-back attitude with Dr. Vath (especially broken-relationship phenomenon). Cherry confessed to relapses. Dr. Vath feels that Hawaii should wait awhile longer. More therapy is his idea, of course. I feel at this point we need more firm directives and less free-form confession of the problems. We already know about the problems. I feel I have reached my saturation point.

I had overdosed on laxatives again and the effects were obvious. Dan was starting to feel despondent about my condition and our relationship. He could not understand why willpower was not sufficient and he hated my dishonesty. He observed a cycle in my behavior patterns and we felt unable to escape its curse. Too obsessed by my pursuit of thinness, I was urged to gain weight and I would eventually comply by consuming huge quantities of high-calorie foods. Then without fail, panic would set in at the thought of putting on the "wrong kind" of weight. Others thought it looked good but all I could see was flab and dimpled fat. Overtaken with fear, I would vomit and shoplift laxatives to remove the added pounds, then lie when confronted about it all. As a result our relationship was undergoing severe strain and Dan still saw me as totally rebellious. Both of us were completely drained, our marriage was being tested to its limits, and our times with Dr. Vath were like lanterns lighting our way in a dark labyrinth. As we left the doctor's office to join Dan's sister Jeanne and her husband, Harris, for dinner, I made a new pledge to feast my way to a healthy weight once again.

A week later Dan discovered me scavenging cookies from the floor of a supermarket while we were shopping. He exploded angrily at my lack of self-control and we stormed at one another all the way home. The incident ended in an emotional outburst and I reached the point of hysteria. Overflowing with guilt and remorse, I ran into the kitchen and seized a butcher knife from a drawer.

"What are you going to do with that?" Dan challenged.

At once, I realized that my self-hatred had finally reached its frenzied but inevitable conclusion. I wanted to kill myself then and there. I didn't know how to be a Christian, a wife, or even a normal human being. And with my recently acquired poundage my self-abhorrence was especially intense. We spent the rest of the evening in deep discussion, prayer, and tears. We tried to hold on until our next appointment.

Thursday, September 15. Dr. Vath's office. As usual Dr. Vath's session was enlightening and encouraging. Cherry's weight is still up (about 111) but she struggles with fears. We talked about a diet for hypoglycemia because sugar addiction is a possibility. Her aches and pains may be attributed to the healing process, as "change causes stress." The problem of control for the mind is a topic these days: open frankness and scheduling time to think over problem areas were two possibilities. Empathy and sharing with a close person were also emphasized. Things are looking better. Positive mental attitude is a must!

"Tell me, Cherry, why is it that you want to die?" Dr. Vath inquired calmly. The question seemed so stark in the peaceful setting of his office with its panoramic view of the city below.

"I don't really think I *do*—I don't know. It's just that sometimes I get so tired, so sick of fighting, so sick of myself. . . ."

"Well, it appears from your behavior that you do, and taking your own life with a knife would just be a speedier, more efficient means of accomplishing what your illness is leading towards. You see, anorexia nervosa may be seen as a slow form of suicide. Although it can begin as a socially acceptable attempt to lose weight, the fear of rejection and guilt over imperfections create a depression and a suicidal plunge that are very difficult to come out of. The potentially lethal partnership of deep depression and low self-esteem is a powerful one."

I had never seen my condition as suicidal before, but I could not escape the reality of Dr. Vath's observations. Whether I wanted to admit it or not, I was gradually killing myself, draining my life away ounce by ounce.

In an effort to redirect my suicidal tendencies into a constructive attitude of self-acceptance, Dan started to tell me several times a day that I was "valuable." Perhaps this approach would keep me alive until I was capable of sustaining myself. Meanwhile, I attempted to follow a diet for hypoglycemics to see if my erratic outbursts were related to biochemical reactions to sugar. At the same time we ended our five-and-one-half month stay in Shelton by moving in with the Ganfields for six weeks before relocating in Hawaii.

My sugar-restricted diet, along with the stress of the temporary move to Seattle, brought me to the point of another regression into laxative abuse and weight loss. What started out as a day of celebrating Dan Ganfield's discharge from the army reserves ended in verbal combat as I shrank to an awful mummylike figure before everyone's eyes during the course of the evening. My panicky denials yielded to the truth only after Dan forced my hand. What followed that night was a kind of group therapy session that included some very insightful input from Dan and Chrissie.

By the end of a marathon meeting that lasted until four in the morning, we had determined how I should focus my energies in coming weeks. We all agreed that I was apparently incapable of seeing myself realistically or of maintaining a consistently healthy diet. Therefore, I needed to trust someone else to help me make food and weight decisions until I could responsibly and logically execute them on my own. We resolved that I should depend on Dan for guidance, support, and reassurance as the pounds crept back onto my body, regardless of the "quality." As a temporary emergency measure, Dan's viewpoint would prevail until I regained my rational capabilities. The true test of my attitude and desire for wellness would be my reactions to Dan's *suggestions,* as he attempted to replace authoritarian commands with gentler alternatives. Thus I would begin to move towards a position of responsible personal recognizance.

As we ended the evening in a chorus of supplication and submission to God in prayer, I haltingly handed Dan the reins of my life.

Thursday, September 29. Dr. Vath meeting. Cherry buoyed greatly as she received (perhaps with a bit too much enthusiasm) the news that her extreme emotional paroxysms could be the result of a need for lithium. Our session was interesting in light of new information on the manic-depressive condition referred to as "mood swing." We went into a second hour (a timely cancellation created more time with Ray) discussing possible book projects. As a writer I

*could assist Ray in publishing some of his excellent therapy
material. I'll listen to the cassette tapes on marriage and
family this Sunday and then we'll begin talking.*

Could it be true? Could my radically changing moods and
behavior actually be the result of something biological? The
thought was encouraging! Perhaps my bad judgment,
impulsiveness, and depression were partly the result of a
physical condition. I was thrilled to think that I may not be
such a terrible person after all!

I began taking lithium carbonate prescribed by Dr. Vath to
stabilize my temperament. This mineral salt would react
with the individual cell membranes, regulating the elec-
trochemical impulses to level out mood swings. People with
bipolar manic-depressive illness experience extreme highs
and lows effecting observable changes in their moods and
behavior. It was not an uncommon phenomenon, Dr. Vath
had explained, and I was in good company with the likes of
Abraham Lincoln and Winston Churchill. Dr. Vath's suggested reading for the topic was *Moodswing,* by Dr. Ronald
Fieve.

That Sunday we went to Dr. Vath's home to pick up the
cassettes Dan needed to listen to in order to begin outlining
a book project based on Dr. Vath's material on marriage and
family therapy. To our surprise, our doctor invited us to join
his family for dinner soon "so that we can get to know one
another better." Interestingly, we found ourselves a bit
reticent to exchange our "omniscient," objective psycho-
therapist for a personal friend. I wondered if I would ever
really be able to relax with him in a nonprofessional setting
without feeling psychologically scrutinized.

Before our next session a landmark in Dan's thinking
about my basic priorities transpired. He and Dan Ganfield

were on a weekend trip that lasted through our second anniversary. I stayed at the apartment with Chrissie because my sister Debby was scheduled to come to Seattle to promote her new record, "You Light Up My Life." During their trip the husbands discussed my anorexia battles at great length and finally concluded that it is possible temporarily to choose against one's own primary motive. For the first time Dan actually realized that I always *wanted* to do the right things even though on occasion I *chose* to do the wrong ones. He came to recognize ambivalence as a legitimate problem to be contended with. It was the best anniversary gift I could have received. At long last Dan, too, began to believe that I really did want to break the chains holding me captive for so many years.

Thursday, October 13. Dr. Vath appointment. We examined progress under the lithium treatment (blood test for Cherry). Progress has been good.

Between our ninth and tenth therapy appointments two interesting developments began to take shape. We started attending a class taught by Dr. Vath at a church on Sunday mornings. Relating to him on a less therapeutic level eased my mind regarding future personal involvements. The second positive influence during this time was the material in the tapes Dan was using to outline a manuscript of Dr. Vath's marriage-therapy techniques.

Dan was impressed with the wisdom and clarity of Dr. Vath's approach to marriage problems and conflict resolution. It was so constructive, so helpful, so right! He began to try applying this new information to our situation, attempting to develop the skills that can sustain a marriage through the inevitable storms. It seemed to be working.

And so was the lithium! Monitoring the level of lithium in my blood helped us to arrive at an appropriate daily dosage. Amazingly, within two weeks Dan was able to see a marked difference in my behavior as a result of a more balanced temperament. The lithium treatment was a kind of stopgap tactic, enabling me to respond to psychotherapy without the distraction of fluctuating emotions. My progress accelerated and after approximately six months, I discontinued my prescription; it was no longer necessary.

The next evening we had our first purely social interaction with Dr. Vath. His wife, Joanne, prepared a delicious dinner and we marveled at the many mutual interests and goals we shared.

Dan felt that the "chemistry" was perfect for their collaboration on the book on marriage. They set up an appointment to discuss their strategy.

After their meeting Dan arrived home to find that I had downed yet another box of laxatives after jogging six miles around Green Lake! What happened?! And why now, just as things were finally looking so positive? It didn't make sense!

But then, when had it ever really made any sense? The only thing to which I could attribute this setback was a binge and subsequent "purge" that occurred the previous night. I had stayed up late after a phone conversation with my parents. I'm not sure what set it off but starting with a small snack, I found myself consuming without thinking until I had become uncomfortable. Had it been a subconscious reaction to the phone call? Instead of reasoning my way through the temptation to throw up, I simply gave in. The next day's jogging and laxative abuse were an extension of the previous night's downfall.

Dan was cool and distant. Resignation and despondency

were settling in like a heavy black cloud. Was it even worth the effort? Was the energy being expended on my anorexia and on our marriage all for nothing? Seeing Dan's emotionless expression motivated me into a rapid weight-gain program to recover the pounds I dropped over the preceding twenty-four hours. Unfortunately the panic I felt at the thought of rejection by Dan resulted in two days of unwise eating, jacking me up to 120 pounds! Although I assured Dan that all was well and under control, I was actually anesthetizing my fear of rejection with a food overdose. My excuses were exposed when I flew into a dither after another phone call from my father.

Daddy called to offer me a television commercial they were planning to tape in a week. He knew we were not earning a regular salary and the combination of making extra money while seeing the family, he thought, would appeal to me. And he was correct. I wanted to do it, but we agreed that Dan and I should consult together before a commitment was made.

When I hung up the phone I was struck with horror at the thought that my parents, not to mention the video cameras, would see me "this heavy." After all, they say that television makes you look ten pounds heavier. I would appear to be 130 pounds! I couldn't live with that. No way!

Dan was fed up. This whole anorexia thing was cumbersome, illogical, and a burden that seemed at times too heavy to bear. Would it ever end? Did he even care anymore?

The following morning, Dan called my dad to explain the potential dangers of my coming down to Los Angeles to do the commercial. He predicted that I would immediately lose weight. Still, consistent with his commitment to let me "do what I would do," he urged me to make my own decision.

As the day of my departure drew near my weight dropped

substantially. Just the prospect of family media involvement
was precipitating a noticeable loss. Dan tried to convince
me to remain at 115 pounds, which still seemed unreason-
ably high to me. In my opinion, he should be happy I wasn't
using laxatives or vomiting to achieve my desired goal.

The day before I was to leave for Los Angeles, the
Ganfields and the O'Neills had another lengthy conversation about my weight. I had lost ten pounds in five days and
I was willing to defend my right to weigh 110 pounds as
long as Dan was willing to challenge it. It was a showdown
of sorts, an emotional arm-wrestling match, and my
obstinance pushed Dan to his limits. After our group
discussion proved fruitless, Dan presented me with the
ultimate choice in the privacy of our room.

"The way I see it," he said with a frigid tone of voice,
"you've got two alternatives. Either you can choose your
family, show biz, and your anorexia, or you can choose me
and the marriage. Do you understand what I'm saying?"

I wasn't quite sure how to answer. I haltingly asked him
to elaborate.

"What I am saying is, think *real* hard before you decide
to come back from L.A. this time. Think *real* hard."

I couldn't believe my ears. He was serious! After all we
had been through he was actually considering throwing in
the towel and admitting defeat. He couldn't! Not now!

It was with great sobriety that I flew down to do the
commercial the next day. I weighed Dan's words heavily
before I left. While I was in Los Angeles I made my choice.

Dan walked up to meet me as I stepped off the return
flight. "Cherry, you look *great!* How did it go in L.A.?"
Dan asked, delighted that I was a little heavier than when I
had left Seattle!

"Well, everything went just fine. I even told Mommy and

Daddy about our plans to settle in the Northwest after Hawaii. They seemed to handle the news quite well!"

Dan put his arm around me and gave me a loving squeeze. I had passed my tests!

Thursday, October 27. Dr. Vath appointment. We talked about Cherry's ideal weight. About 115? We concluded that we shouldn't set rigid numbers. Cherry's recent talks with her parents show new openness developing. This will probably be our last appointment for a while as L.A. and Hawaii draw closer. The Seattle option looks good. I am happy with Cherry's progress—some "hiding" syndrome remains, but her desire seems set towards openness. God, in faith, I continue to receive Your help, wisdom, healing.

At the time of our eleventh and final appointment with Dr. Vath, Dan and I were planning to be in Hawaii for a month or two at the most, after which we were to settle in the Seattle area. We did not realize that this would be our last real therapy session, so there was no celebration or special goodbye. Instead, we focused on the skills we had learned and would certainly continue to need in resolving conflict within our marriage.

"How would you define love?" Dr. Vath asked the leading question.

"Wishing someone their highest good," Dan replied.

"Being willing to lay your life down for another person," I suggested.

"My definition of love is caring as much about someone else's well-being and security as your own. Sound familiar? It's a little like doing unto others as you would have them do to you, or like loving your neighbor as yourself. My definition certainly isn't original—someone else 'published first,' a couple thousand years ago.''

We all smiled as the doctor continued.

"How about marriage? How would you define marriage, Dan?"

"A union of two people who decide to leave their families and start one of their own," Dan answered.

"That's basically right, but there's a little bit more to it, I think. I see marriage as a *process* in which there is a blending together of two lives that are different into a working unit that allows each individual to develop their potential to its optimum level."

Again we smiled in approval of Dr. Vath's insight and proceeded to review the developmental phases a marriage inevitably experiences, including the storms. We talked about love, honesty, and empathy as being essential ingredients in any successful marriage as well as the tools that can be applied in resolving conflict.

"I had an interesting experience in my Sunday-morning class when I was sharing these ideas," Dr. Vath related. "A gentleman asked me which of the three ingredients—love, honesty, or empathy—was the most important. I answered with the question, 'Which leg of a three-legged stool is the most important?' A very wise man in the back of the room answered, 'The one that's missing!' "

And so, on November 11, we left Seattle for Los Angeles to spend the Thanksgiving holiday with my family before departing for Hawaii. I was filled with anticipation and excitement about the road ahead. There was a growing inner confidence, burning like a flame, enabling me to see more clearly as I emerged gradually from the darkness of disease. I had even begun to feel the reality of my value as a person—and as a woman. I likened myself to an intricately designed, fine gold chain that had become badly tangled in knots. Dr. Vath had helped me straighten the chain, and together Dan and I were beginning to untie the knots. I had come so close to throwing it all away, but I finally realized—and just in time—that the chain had never lost its original value merely because it was tangled. Ultimately I had recognized my worth as an individual and, at age twenty-three, was eager to carve out an identity for myself independently of my parents, my sisters, and even Dan. I was anxious to find out after all these years, "Who is this Cherry, anyway?"

CHAPTER NINE

Cherry Blossoms

Our two months in Hawaii turned into two years. Once we arrived, Dan and I believed that this hardworking, Christian community nestled in the cradle of tropical paradise would be the perfect "next step" in our journey together. Not only would we be on our own away from our families, but it would afford me the opportunity to blossom as an individual.

The environment was both beautiful and relaxing, the waves rhythmically slapping expanses of smooth sand or crashing against lava rocks, occasionally lulling us into a state of euphoria. When we landed at the Kona airport that kind of total relaxation in a setting of sunbathed beaches, blue skies, and sea breezes was just the medicine we needed. In fact, our time in Hawaii proved to be a sort of continuation of therapy.

Once the vacation was over we made a decision to move to Hawaii for an indefinite stay. Play was done and work began. As staff members living in the Kona Village community, we had to earn our keep like everyone else. At first I reacted negatively to the structure of life in the community: working from eight o'clock until five on top of rotated duties of food preparation, kitchen cleanup, office and switchboard work, scheduled community meals, and numerous group meetings for spiritual or business purposes. This left precious little time to pursue personal activities like jogging and other exercising, which were still at the top of my list of daily priorities. Still, I needed to follow the policy to be legitimately "on staff," so I started out cautiously, assuming only a part-time eight-to-two shift at the "Wee Care" day-care center for children ages three to five.

After one week I had forgotten my frustrations and looked forward to my interaction with the Kona kids. It was certainly the right place for me to begin gradually directing my attention outward. I had been so introspective for so long that I had nearly lost touch with the satisfaction of helping others. It was marvelous, and what better recipients than an assortment of happy, energetic, carefree children. As long as they felt my love and concern for them I could do no wrong in their eyes. And the love I received in return was the best possible prescription for someone with low self-esteem. I think the children helped me more than I could ever have helped them.

My next job was to assist the manager of our community's general store, called "The Captain's Porthole." I started as a cashier, then learned how to do the bookkeeping. When the woman managing the operation had to return to her home in Australia, I was left with the full responsibility of management. I did all of the buying and stocking, most of the cashiering, all of the accounting, as well as ordering books and record albums. I even helped plan the expansion of the store, which included tearing down walls, redecorating, and adding a frozen-yogurt machine!

While I was managing the Porthole, I also began work on a children's musical in collaboration with Jimmy and Carol

Owens, an expert team of songwriters who specialize in Christian material. They had recently moved to Hawaii from Los Angeles, where we had known one another through business and church associations. Together we wrote a musical fantasy with a moral, about a village of ants dealing with their own "prodigal son." *Ants' hillvania* was finally recorded and released by Sparrow Records and was nominated for a Grammy Award in the children's music category.

Step by step, day by day, I was learning to approach and conquer ever more creative projects. The greatest expression of the creativity that had seemed dead during the darkest years of my struggles with anorexia nervosa was displayed in the spring of 1979. Responding to a request for singers to participate in the chorus of an upcoming Easter drama, I suddenly found myself in charge of casting and directing the whole production. Then I took on the role of choreographer, produced special effects in makeup and lighting, dabbled in costuming, oversaw the construction of props, and wrote the script for the narrator. Our Easter Passion play was a resounding success. My only regret is that we neglected to videotape the performance. It would have rivaled many professional stage productions, in spite of our limited resources. It was a wonderfully enriching experience and revealed to me talents and capabilities I had never recognized.

During all of my activities Dan was busy at work as well. He established and directed a graphics department at the Hawaii base and personally designed almost all of the art work emanating from the Kona community for the two years we were there. In what spare time he had, he completed the book on marriage that he and Dr. Vath had discussed. It was published by Winston Press, Minneapolis, Minnesota, and is entitled *Marrying for Life*.

As Dan continued his research and writing on Dr. Vath's marriage concepts, we were able to redefine our own marriage roles. Instead of Dan assuming a position of preeminence in the decision-making process, we became equals. When faced with a conflict, a problem, or a decision, we worked collaboratively to reach a point of mutual agreement that would meet the needs of both parties. And our marriage relationship grew increasingly stronger as we pursued the development of those three special ingredients—love, honesty, and empathy.

Whether Dan and I had ever actually stopped loving one another I don't know. There were times when both of us wanted to escape from the other—those bleak nights of despair when it seemed all hope was lost. But one thing I do know for certain is that we never gave up our commitment to one another no matter how horrible things appeared to be. Once we knew what love really was we extended our understanding of it to every area of our lives: we cared for one another as we cared for ourselves. We had stuck it out together and now our love was deeper and stronger than ever.

Dan truly began to develop compassion during our months on the island. He started trying to understand why I did the things I did and how I felt about them rather than dismissing them as bizarre, neurotic aberrations. And even I was able to empathize with Dan as I tried to imagine myself as the husband of an anoretic wife. From his vantage point I could see reasons for outrage, attempts at authoritarianism, and desperation. In fact, when I look back over the years of hell we endured after our optimistic, idealistic wedding, I find myself amazed at his self-control and restraint.

Understanding what Dan had felt motivated me to greater honesty. I had become a chronic liar when it came to the subjects of food, diet, exercise, vomiting, laxatives, and all the rest. Lying had become a way of life for me—a deeply ingrained habit, almost an involuntary reflex. Knowing that it was wrong to lie had not been as strong an influence as my desire to be thin at any cost, even the cost of broken or debilitated relationships. Now with clearer thinking and altered priorities, I was able to work towards complete openness, honesty, and transparency on all levels and on every subject. There was a real sense of remorse on both sides as we realized how inappropriate and unloving we had been and we worked hard together towards individual and marital growth.

But there were still moments of stress and strain over occasional manifestations of my dying disorder. When responsibilities loomed before me like villains too numerous and too large for me to handle, I lapsed into brief anoretic phases. The laxative abuse or vomiting would return like a conditioned response but never to the point of enslavement. Their emergence just served as a reminder to be aware of the remnants of the illness.

The lengthiest of these replayed episodes of the long-running nightmare began with the filming of the first of four Boone family television specials on ABC. It was to be a "Springtime Special" coinciding with the Easter and Passover holidays of 1978. Returning to Hollywood, my family, the old house, the media involvement with its long hours and multifaceted pressures—all of it at once was more than I could cope with and I lost so much weight that Daddy was willing to sacrifice my participation if my health was being threatened by it. Needless to say, I wasn't about to default again so I managed to recover the lost pounds in time for the taping. The wheels of worry, fueled by old fears, had, however, been set in motion and I battled the familiar tendencies and self-destructive habits for the four months that followed. My weight fluctuated between 90 and 100 pounds.

In August, Mommy came to visit us in Hawaii. I was in the throes of striving to stay in control of my condition when she arrived. In fact I was the worst I had been in weeks, calling back the haunting images of protruding bones and hollowed cavities. To my amazement, my mother's reaction was not the usual anxiety over my health, but rather a positive, peaceful transcendence above the fear and concern that normally plagued her when she saw me so thin. It was as if something had liberated her. During her one-week stay Mommy explained to me the reasons for her new tranquility.

She had been alone at the Beverly Hills home for most of the summer and had taken advantage of her solitude to pursue a program of diet, exercise, and relaxation. I was so impressed by her trimmer body and more confident demeanor that I asked her for more details. Her approach involved a ten-to-twenty minute period of total relaxation every day in which the technique of visualization, or guided imagery, played a major role. This prayerful "meditation" time, along with an exercise to promote the development of self-love, had been the two most important factors in her transformation.

After Mommy left I started practicing her techniques. Every day for approximately one month I set aside a time to meditate, to relax, to visualize, and to pray. In a dark and quiet setting I would lie on my back and concentrate on relaxing every muscle of my body. Then I visualized myself in an open field or floating on a raft down a shaded stream to enhance the relaxation. Once I was totally peaceful I would guide my mind's eye over every inch of my physical frame, "seeing" myself at an ideal, healthy, and well-toned weight. I imagined stepping on the scale and seeing the needle fluctuate between 113 and 118 pounds, and then sitting down to eat nutritional foods while turning away others that would be unhealthy or threatening to me.

The results after only three weeks of this simple practice were almost unbelievable! I looked and felt better physically and emotionally than I had since my early teens. I weighed in at a healthy 114 pounds by the time Dan and I flew to Los Angeles to participate in our family's second television special.

With each successive visit to Beverly Hills, my ability to maintain my new identity in the old environment grew. Or, as Dr. Vath might have put it, I was playing a new role on the old stage. My weight never again made the frightening plunge below 100 pounds and my relationships with members of my family improved tremendously. As I learned during my discussions with my sisters and parents, I was not the only one who had been affected by the pressures of both Hollywood and family life. At one point or another, each of us had faced challenges wherein the stakes were high and the choices critical. Their decisions, like my own, had not always been the best. Though I felt sorrow for their struggles, I was able to see that all of us act and react inappropriately at times. We all have our own times of "craziness."

During the taping of our fourth and final television special, a monumental development took place in terms of family dynamics. My mother was becoming extremely concerned about some of my behavior that she was wrongly interpreting as anoretic. She was paying for me to receive regular massages from a professional who felt she could stimulate my menstrual cycle through acupressure. The masseuse also gave me some nutritional advice that I began to follow in hopes of regaining a healthy reproductive system. When my weight took a dip Mommy began to worry.

"I should never have set up those appointments with Annette," she said as the conversation heated up. We had been working at ABC all day and had just arrived home after a grueling taping session at the studio. Mommy followed me into the kitchen where I was in the process of searching the cabinets for something that might strike my fancy. Exhausted and hungry, the last thing I wanted to hear was advice. But Mommy continued.

"It just looks like you're getting worse instead of better!"

"That's a bunch of bullcrap!" I replied, jerking open the cabinet next to the sink.

To my surprise, Mommy bolted across the room, slammed the cabinet shut, and shouted, "Don't you *ever* talk like that to me in *my* house! Do you hear me?"

My shock at her reaction put me on the defensive. I was still being expected to behave as the "dutiful daughter" when I was under my parents' roof. I felt as if my hard-earned independence was being challenged with each visit. Finally I erupted.

"When are you going to stop treating me like a child? Why can't you relate to me as an adult?! I'm twenty-four years old and even though I'll always be your daughter, I'm *not* a baby anymore!"

I did it! I actually said what I felt for years but could never reveal. I declared my independence, embraced my adulthood, and confronted my mother with a truth to which both of us had been blind. The little bird who fought so furiously—and belatedly—to learn to fly refused to have her wings clipped.

Afterwards, Mommy and I discussed the incident. We apologized for losing our tempers—I assured Mommy that I meant no harm. I was sorry if I hurt her and I agreed to be more careful with my vocabulary. She acknowledged that I had been right: I was an adult, and she would try to treat me as such.

Our love for one another was reaffirmed and even transformed. The umbilical cord had finally been cut and we were free to be peers—to be friends. To this day I see that kitchen encounter as a painful but necessary event in my healing. It represents my disengagement from the enmeshing network of the family as well as the beginning of a new process of relating to my parents in an appropriate and more fulfilling way. My relationship with them and my sisters today is better than it ever was.

And my feelings about myself have improved immensely, partly the result of another very effective practice Mommy shared with me during the trip to Hawaii. She told me how a particular mental exercise had helped her in her growth towards self-acceptance and suggested again that it might do the same for me. So, along with the relaxation and imagery, I began to look at myself in the mirror when I woke up and again just before bed. Fixing my stare squarely at my own eyes, I repeated aloud several times, "I love myself unconditionally."

At first, I felt foolish—I even laughed. Who did I think I was kidding? But gradually, as I followed through with the procedure on a regular basis, I began to mean what I was saying. I could honestly feel the love for myself filling me with a warmth and happiness that could not be contained. It naturally spilled over into a general sense of goodwill towards those around me. The doctor was right again! By learning to love myself, I was finally able to begin genuinely loving others.

Interestingly, it was while we were in Los Angeles for the last television special that an opportunity arose for me to undertake a sort of symbolic penance—something to redeem the wasted years of my life. In response to the refugee crisis in Cambodia, my parents hosted a gathering of some of the foremost leaders in Christian relief, media, and ministry in their home. Dan organized the meeting with only ten days' notice and, incredibly, almost everyone invited was able to attend. A new organization called Save The Refugees Fund was born and Dan was selected to be the executive director with Daddy as honorary chairman. It was designed to channel emergency financial aid to voluntary agencies meeting the needs of refugee populations through food and medical relief and to encourage development. Rather than form another agency and cope with administrative headaches and hassles, Dan would research the agencies in place, document their projects to be certain of their efficiency and cost-effectiveness, and raise funds to be dispersed as a means of fueling the lifesaving machinery geared to help the homeless, poor, and hungry of the world.

Dan's new position necessitated a move back to the mainland and, after two years away, we settled in Seattle the last week of 1979. Since then Dan has been quite successful in his fund-raising efforts. Save The Refugees Fund has helped homeless and hungry people in Asia, Africa, Central America, and even the United States. And, irony of ironies, an ex-victim of starvation is now involved in helping those who are starving by no choice of their own.

Our move to Seattle in 1979 was followed by the purchase of our first home in the spring of 1980. At last, after five and a half years of marriage, we had a place of our own. It was like retracing our steps in a new and positive light.

Another form of development that Dan and I experienced was in the spiritual arena. On the eve of Easter 1981, we entered the Catholic Church. After seven years of personal religious studies, Dan decided to enter the catechumenate, a course of instruction that culminates in baptism and/or confirmation into the Catholic Church. When Dan began his classes, I joined him to better understand his spiritual leanings. For the sake of unity, I chose to attend with an open mind; but for the sake of integrity, I would not have followed Dan on this new path unless I personally agreed with what I learned, feeling assured that the new step would be God's will for *me* as well.

With Dan's extensive study of his deeply held Christian faith and my intuitive grasp of sacramental theology, we were ultimately able to realize the universal message of a traditional Protestant hymn: just as many are the roads that lead to the same mountaintop, many are the paths that lead to the one Christ. And this new but well-traveled path we would choose was simply the one whose particular signs and symbols most clearly pointed the way for *us* at this particular stage on our spiritual journey towards the God in whom all men and women, no matter what their religion, "live and move and have their being."

The interior development that has taken place in our lives has not at all alienated us from our Protestant backgrounds. Indeed, we feel an unbreakable and loving bond with the faith of our younger years. Without having been where we were—the right place at the right time for us then—we would not be where we are now—the right place at the right time for us at this particular moment in eternity. Both paths form a crossroad of faith where truth and love join together in the form of a cross that heals and reveals, with no trace of conflict, pride, or regret. Like so much of life, spiritual growth is a continuum, a dynamic *process,* a never-ending journey toward individual understanding of who we really are in the eyes of Christ and of how the Light of the World expects each of us to shine at every new and precious moment. Like all Christians, we have so much to learn— but it's coming, and through the grace of God our relationship with Him continues and grows. We are thankful for every yesterday, today, and tomorrow.

It was in church one Sunday morning, in the middle of our catechumenate studies, that Dan and I, independently of one another, prayed for a child. Neither of us mentioned it to the other until two months later, I discovered I was pregnant! On January 9, 1981, it was confirmed: Dan and I were going to be parents after more than six years of marriage. I had not resumed menstruation until the preceding autumn, and after only three full cycles I had conceived. As Dan and I divulged our secret prayers we knew they had been speedily and wondrously answered.

Following a lovely, normal, problem-free pregnancy, and only three and a half hours of labor during natural childbirth, Brittany Ann Boone O'Neill was born as healthy as could be. It was Thursday, August 20, 1981, at 8:14 P.M. in Bellevue, Washington.

Brittany has been a delight to Dan and me, with a cheery disposition and beautiful, delicate features. She is a good baby, easy to care for and even easier to love. I nursed her from the very beginning and her health has been excellent, her growth and development perfectly normal. But in her normalcy there is a special message for me from the "Master Designer." With Brittany's birth I felt that God was giving me His official stamp of approval on my recovery. In a sense He was saying to me, "Okay, Cherry, you have proven that you can be responsible for your own life. Now I can trust you with another one."

As I conclude my tale of struggles and victory I want to address myself to the many others who share my plight. My story ends happily, and for that I am very grateful. I have told it to groups of anoretics, their loved ones, and others. I have even been involved in some therapy sessions assisting Dr. Vath and have helped him with a presentation on anorexia nervosa at the University of Washington School of Medicine. I am glad to offer hope to any who feel the hopelessness I once felt.

However, in the writing of this book I would be making a serious mistake not to mention some of the risks and consequences of anorexia nervosa. Statistics report a 15 to 20 percent mortality rate for victims of this disease, who are no longer limited to upper-middle-class adolescent females. I have met children under the age of ten and adults above the age of forty who have developed the disorder. I believe the incidence in males will continue to increase, although with the phenomenal increase in female sufferers, the more than ten-to-one ratio of women to men may not be radically altered. Of the 80 percent who survive, it is said one third remain chronically anoretic, checking in and out of hospitals indefinitely. A second third walk a tightrope between relapse and recovery—borderline anoretic throughout their lives. The final third recovers.

Obviously, I count myself very fortunate, but my goal is

to see these statistics change. I firmly believe that with the increasing knowledge of this illness, along with the development of more effective therapeutic techniques, the disease can be conquered.

Amazingly, I suffered little physical damage in the long run. I must have come from sturdy stock to have endured the abuse I leveled at myself. The gastrointestinal problems I had developed during my anoretic years decreased to practically nothing while I was pregnant. I eat fiber and chew an occasional antacid tablet, but beyond that, all is well. The problem of amenorrhea was rectified by the resumption of my reproductive cycle and the birth of our daughter. With my dissolving teeth I was not quite so lucky: I recently completed the crowning of twenty teeth. But, in view of other consequences, ten thousand dollars worth of dental work is a relatively small price to pay to overcome the effects of anorexia.

Dying from malnutrition is not the only risk of an anoretic or bulimaretic (binge/purge) lifestyle. There have been many cases of ruptured stomach and esophagus, severe dehydration, rupturing of internal membranes, gastritis, ulcers, vagal-nerve block, irritable-bowel syndrome, bowel tumors, megacolon, intestinal infection, ruptured facial blood vessels, "insulin dump" (from sugar binges), hypoglycemia, chronic sinusitis, kidney damage, bleeding and infection of the throat, endocrine problems, abnormal metabolism, and severe electrolyte imbalances, which can lead to various neuromuscular problems, including muscle spasms, cardiac arrest, and death.

Anorexia nervosa and its related disorders are serious illnesses that require expert attention. My purpose is not to frighten someone with anorexia—shock therapy does not necessarily keep an anoretic alive. But it might motivate a suffering person to look for help—the right kind of help.

I believe that an individual with anorexia nervosa needs to seek professional psychotherapy—not just because that is what helped me in my recovery, but because it is a psychosomatic disorder. It is an illness that starts in the emotions and the psyche and grows like a cancer until it finally manifests itself observably in the body and in behavior. A competent counselor for both the anoretic and her family is the best prescription I can offer, along with tapping into support groups, ground therapy, and a network of newsletters that are springing up across the country.

My story is one of hope—hope that against all odds answers can be found, solutions can be discovered, conflicts can be resolved. It is a story of faith—faith in those who love you regardless of what you do, faith in yourself (even when it is only the size of a mustard seed), and faith in a God who offers us life when death is all around us.

Finally, my story is one of *process*—the process of maturing into a responsible adult, of recovering from a complicated disorder one step at a time, of reconciliation in marriage and spirituality. Our world is geared towards instant success and quick fixes. But my anorexia was like a huge steamship barreling towards a waterfall. When the orders came to make a 180-degree turn away from destruction, it was as if the ship's wheel was locked. Therapy gave me the keys and, with them in hand, I set myself on a course leading to life instead of death. But I had to realize, as did Dan, that the speed, momentum, and size of the steamship would require time to make it turn—the turning would be a *process*. And so we learned about patience . . . and about love.

With the ordeal of anorexia nervosa behind us, Dan and Brittany and I are living in health, happiness, and love, awaiting the next step in our journey together. To quote someone who published first, "In short, there are three things that will last: faith, hope and love; and the greatest of these is love" (I Corinthians 13:13).

Letters to Our Daughter
Shirley and Pat Boone

DEAREST CHERRY:

Your book has caused many emotions to surface and many memories to stir—memories of my sixteen-year-old mother giving birth to me, my childhood perceptions of life with my parents, and as a teenager who lost her mother to an early death, coping with the blessings and problems of having a famous father until his death in 1968.

Thoughts of holding a two-year-old in my arms in wet towels for three days and nights to try to get your temperature, which ranged between 105 and 107 degrees, back to normal—only to finally have to put you in a hospital—watch them strap you down in a crib and stick needles in your legs to give you fluid—then to be sent home without you.

How many times did I say to you girls, "Get something on your feet" as you entered the kitchen with its cold vinyl floor. Then when the umpteenth time you walked in, I said, "Cherry, please put something on your feet!" you threw that foot up in my face with "something" written on the sole. We laughed at the way your mind worked!

We worked on so many school assignments together and

on many other projects—memories we don't have time or space to share.

Then came those years when the laughing ceased with the seriousness of your mind being consumed by a new thinking pattern which I never understood. All I knew was the heart of that young girl I nursed, laughed with, worked with, and loved more than my own life—so my prayers were constantly "Rewire her thinking, Lord!"

You have been rewired, honey, and the grace of God once again prevails in our lives—but just as you went through your pain to bring Brittany into this world and just as you hold that precious little girl in your arms and you can't even remember the pain—that's how the pain came for me, in waves, raising you girls—pain that's soon forgotten because of the joy.

The Bible says *love* covers a multitude of sin—yours and ours! My love for you causes my memories to go back to the joy more than the pain. Raising you girls has helped me better understand my parents and better understand how God must look at all His children.

We never claimed to be perfect parents and we know you girls were not perfect children—but we all have a perfect Savior and because of Him, I see you through eyes of love and can hardly remember the pain! I hope the same will be true for you. I just thank God *you're well* and remind you once again—

I'll always love you,
MOMMY

DEAR MUGWUMPS:

I've just been reading over your manuscript, and I have this giant lump in my throat that won't go away. My eyes are brimming and my heart is full—full of pain reopened and reexperienced, full of love and gratitude for the way things have worked out, and full of deep pride in you and the way you've told this remarkable story. I wonder if I can possibly express the way your Mama and I feel right now. As you know, when you were born, she and I were barely twenty years old!

I'm so glad you can understand how we felt, two kids fresh out of our teens ourselves, with our own little real-life doll. You have your own little Brittany now, but you were twenty-seven when she was born, and you and Dan had lived as adult man and wife for years before she came.

Picture two kids from Nashville transplanted in Denton, Texas, the "Daddy" a sophomore in college and the "Mommy" a nurse trainee, who suddenly had their own little miracle, their own tiny "Extra-Terrestrial," another human *life* to care for, to raise and teach and feed and clothe and nurse and protect and help to grow into young womanhood herself! We were awestruck; we were thrilled and numb at once; we were completely entranced and enthralled with you, but also weak-kneed and wondering as we looked into your trusting angel eyes and faced the incredible responsibility you represented.

Could we possibly do it?

Could two naïve, inexperienced though well-meaning young *kids* actually learn about parenting quickly enough to get you started successfully on your own life, help you find out and develop who you are and are supposed to be, protect you from the blundering and traumatic mistakes that almost all parents make, and nurture that bubbling innocent joy in you until you could develop wisdom and judgment and character to go with it?

We determined that, with God's help, we'd do it.

We got down on our knees and prayed fervently. We asked God who gave you to us to help us be good parents; we committed you into His care; we vowed to do our dedicated best to be what you needed and deserved, to train and love and cherish and protect you with every resource we had or would have, to help you know who God was and how He wanted you to live, to be the best real friends a baby girl could hope to have.

We loved you so much—and we knew that meant we'd have to learn how to say no sometimes.

That, we found, can be the hardest part of all.

From the very beginning, you were so pert and perky, so aware and interested in everything around you, so irresistibly cute and winning in your reactions to people that *every*body wanted to hold you, to enjoy you, to spark and hold your attention, just as we did. And, like all babies, you ate it up!

But then came bedtime. *That* you didn't like at all.

Before you were six months old, bedtime brought on our first heartache, the first real clash of wills between young parents and adored child. And that's what it was—an amazing demonstration of your will. We knew you were full and dry and well, that it was past the time for you to be asleep, that you'd had an active day with lots of attention and affection, and that you were physically tired. But you just didn't want to give up and go to sleep; we'd take turns patting your back and trying to get you to lie still just long enough for nature to lull you into blissful unconsciousness, but just when we thought you were "out," you'd stir, lift your head and chortle and babble some garbled version of "I'm still awake! Keep rubbing! Don't go away! Better yet, why don't we forget this sleep business and go in the other room, so I can see what you're up to?"

I guess all parents have been through their versions of this, but it was our first time, and we wanted to do it right. So eventually, we decided we'd *have* to let you fret and cry yourself to sleep, that we couldn't let you have your way forever, no matter how cute you were. We were aware of the biblical admonition to "train up a child in the way he should go: and when he is old, he will not depart from it" (Proverbs 22:6) and that in the same place it warns "foolishness is bound in the heart of a child; but the rod of correction shall drive it far from him" (Proverbs 22:15). We certainly weren't ready to take a rod to you, but we felt we owed it to you to let you cry awhile, if that was what it took to convince you to trust us about your bedtime, to get you to yield to what was best for you.

But we weren't ready for your determination!

I wish you could journey back in a time machine and watch Shirl and me verbally wrestling with each other, first one holding the other back, and then the reverse. You'd cry and cry and cry, angry sometimes and pleading sometimes and apparently choking sometimes—those were the worst moments; one or both of us would rush in and pick you up, and *instantly* you'd be fine, laughing and bright-eyed and ready to get up. You'd won! And you could keep it up for hours! We couldn't believe your endurance, your stamina, your will power!

And that's what made it so rough for us, your Mama and me. See, it wasn't just a question of your bedtime, or even your physical health; it was a matter of who was going to "call the shots." It had become a contest of wills. It would have been far easier for us to just give in, but we felt that, for your sake, this was a contest you needed to lose.

In a couple of months, you got the message. And were we grateful, for lots of reasons. Your sister Linda was already on the way!

Right after Linda, there was Debby, and then Laury. In fact, by the time you were three-and-a-half years old, you had three little sisters—and your Mom and I were just twenty-three years old! Talk about a crash course in parenting; we were going for our Ph.D.s and could barely read and write! Ironically, I *was* in college all this time, and when I graduated from Columbia University in 1958, in a class that included several thousand others, I was the only one with four children and a wife tagging along. It made the papers everywhere, largely because my singing career had taken off and the public seemed interested in this college kid who was juggling hit records, television, and movies with church, school, and marriage—and having a baby a year! It *was* quite a story, and you were right in the middle of it.

You and your sisters were on the covers of all the magazines, on television with me once in a while, were recognized frequently in public places, and you all came to sense soon enough (too soon, we felt) that others considered you something special. During that time, you developed the very touching attitude of a little "Assistant Mama," often cautioning your sisters and protecting them and trying to see that they did what they were supposed to do. Your Mom, with all she had to do, appreciated the help, and we both marveled at your growing sense of responsibility, your earnest desire to please and help.

And what fun we had!

Remember Disneyland, when we all disguised ourselves

and spent two hilarious, giddy days completely anonymous? Remember the train rides and the cross-country trips as a family in the station wagon, stopping when and where we pleased and moving on just as people would start to recognize us? Remember when we took a house outside London when I was filming there and Mommy actually took you girls to see the Queen one rainy day? Remember the countless hours I made up stories with you girls, each of us taking turns as the storyteller, about four adventurous young tykes named Flopsy, Mopsy, Cottontail, and Rocky (who bore suspicious resemblances to Cherry, Lindy, Debby, and Laury)?

Remember catching your first fish in Florida? Remember picnics and children's matinees and Sunday school and endless hours of working together on your homework, the bedtime talks and hugs and prayers, the rides on tandem bikes and motorcycles and sitting in my lap, "learning to drive"? Oh, boy. . . .

Of course, some things you probably couldn't remember, like the after-midnight hours Mommy and I spent assembling Christmas toys and Halloween costumes (surely the most elaborate ever), and early Easter mornings when we hid the eggs all over the yard for you girls and your friends to find in just a few frantic, screaming minutes. You probably wouldn't have known then about the all-night "red eye" flights I took home so I could be with you and Mommy at the school functions. The important thing was that we were there, together, as a family.

But I'm sure you do remember the love, the involvement, the desire we all had to know each other and to care and share together, even during the time you described so poignantly when Shirley and I somehow drifted apart. Even then, when we were so "out of sync" with each other, you remember we tried to keep communicating with you girls, tried to keep home life as "normal" for you as possible; a losing battle, under those circumstances of course, but you remember the efforts. And I remember your efforts to help and to please, even then.

That's why the makeup conflict came as such a shock to me, and why I may have over-reacted. When you began to wear what seemed garish, unbecoming and exaggerated eye shadows and lipsticks and rouges to school and to church, I first kidded, then reasoned, and finally ordered you to check all makeup with your Mom before you left the house. When you didn't, or when you left home one way and came home another, obviously determined not to obey—it *was* a shock. This didn't seem like you to me, and I felt I had to be very firm again, because (like the bedtime incidents so long before) it had become something other than a matter of makeup or taste—it was now a conflict of will, with three younger sisters looking on.

I hated it, and I still do. I wish I had just ignored the makeup situation, realizing you'd grow out of it. But remember, you were our first—we wanted so much to do right by you, and for you, and your sisters were crowding right on your heels, watching and waiting for clues to guide *their* choices. So we seemed trapped in a showdown, in another contest you couldn't afford to win, at least in my view. It was exasperating for both of us, and for your Mom, who was caught in the middle, but we lived through it. Gradually, you toned down your makeup, and the problem seemed to be resolved.

All of this was crucial to your Mom and me because you girls were rapidly arriving at the dating age, and we knew that if we didn't keep trust and communication and practical and *spiritual* guidelines alive then, the whole ballgame would be lost, and the happiness and growth that we'd all put so much of ourselves into would dissolve and disintegrate into teenage trauma, tragedy, and heartbreak. After all the years of training and involvement and growing together, one major mistake in an unguarded moment could change your life forever, and wreak emotional and spiritual damage that a lifetime might not repair. You were now only three or four years away from the age your Mom and I were when you were born! We had so little time left, it seemed, to be everything to you, for you, that we felt you deserved, that we'd promised we'd be and do for you.

As much or more than anything else, it was this realization that brought your Mom and me to a new spiritual commitment. We became painfully, starkly aware that we didn't have the answers you needed, that we didn't have the wisdom in ourselves to guide you and your sisters the rest of the way to happy womanhood, through the treacherous amoral environment of Hollywood. We needed help; divine help, we sought it—and it was there! You've recounted, briefly, how this turnaround came about and the effect it had on all of us, on the marriage and our family and each of us individually. It was startling, it was dramatic, it was powerful, and it happened just in time. We thought we "had it made" then.

Enter anorexia.

Trouble in paradise.

Oh, our lives weren't paradise, but at least they now had real purpose and direction; there were discoverable answers to the problems; we were united as a family again, and there was world-wide demand for what we had to offer—the picture of a family that really enjoyed being a family, that loved each other and worked together for the common good, that boldly underscored traditional values and spiritual principles, that proved this "family thing" still works.

We all went on television a lot together, and one of the most memorable moments was on a Merv Griffin show when he asked you girls, "Now come on, Boones, level with me—with your parents' strict guidelines, don't you honestly feel you're missing out on some things?" And you, Cherry, shot back, "Yes sir—*trouble*. Lots of trouble."

From your friends' experiences, you knew what you were talking about, and from the audience's enthusiastic applause, you knew that many agreed with what you said. You knew you were right, you knew we were "bustin' our buttons" with pride in you. You knew you had represented all of us perfectly.

But none of us, including you, knew you were beginning to starve to death.

And why?

After all this time, after all the tears and aches and anger and prayer and study and trials, after reading your own brilliant account of those years right up to today, I can only guess.

I think it comes down to *twin forces, of almost equal intensity*, operating in you and in opposition to each other, but each tied to your exceptional intelligence and unusually strong willpower. You wanted to please us, to fulfill the expectations of all who really mattered to you, to be exemplary in every way; you really did—and still do. And at the same time, you were ferociously determined to gain absolute control over your body, your appearance, your sense of personal well-being, no matter what the cost or methods. Eventually, when the two desires met on a collision course, you weren't willing to give either one up—

and so they nearly tore you apart. In bitter irony, as you so terribly detail, the desire for absolute mastery turned you into a helpless slave.

I surely don't believe you started out to starve yourself. I don't believe you meant to rebel against your Mom and Dad or create a dilemma in which you had to constantly choose whether to please us or yourself. I believe it started as innocently as your tearful demands from your crib in Denton, Texas, and your early teen attempts at glamour through makeup—very understandable, common attempts to accomplish personal goals without much regard for parental "druthers." Everybody, every family goes through that.

What really set you apart, what made your reaction to our rather ordinary family priorities and guidelines so different from your three sisters', was the growing intensity of your twin goals *and* your intelligence and will.

Oh, the other girls dreamed up all kinds of ways to get around the rules, in relatively harmless escapades, and I had real head-to-head run-ins with each of them from time to time. Each girl had intelligence and will of her own, and gradually asserted healthy independence without too much overt rebellion—love and understanding eventually winning over all. But none of them was willing to work a *fraction* as hard as you, with anything like the steely, almost frightening determination to calculate, to calibrate, to regulate every calorie, every ounce, every second. And when all doors seemed closed, when every healthy method was ruled out, your intelligence allowed you to devise some incredible complex scheme—and your fierce will enabled you to tunnel around or through the obstacle to your goal, the imagined triumph of perfection.

The Bible describes rebellion as "the sin of witchcraft."

Though I *know* you didn't intend to rebel against us, and certainly not God—you consciously and continually approved and agreed with our reasonings and priorities—you gradually developed a private goal that set you again on a collision course with us. And you knew, from past experience, you couldn't win head-on. So, a double life began, a secretive, convoluted, distorted, and ultimately destructive existence that utilized your very intelligence and will to nearly rob you of life—and us of our cherished and precious daughter, a wellspring of our joy and life.

Cherry, I know you never intended any of this trauma, and you know neither did we. I know you tell your story in painful and intimate detail in the hope that others may escape the full measure of sorrow and anguish we all went through together, you and Dan and Shirley and I and your sisters and friends. You know how much you have been loved, how deeply and completely, since God first handed you to two agonizingly inexperienced young kids twenty-eight years ago, and you know how proud we are of you and how grateful we are that God has brought you literally through "the valley of the shadow of death" and caused you to lie down by the still waters, has anointed your head with oil and prepared a table before you in the presence of your enemies.

As evidence of the shepherd's rod and staff, you and Dan now have your own little "Extra-Terrestrial" life to shape and guide and marvel over. Your Mom and I know, with the lumps in our throats, how much you both intend for little Brittany, and we've already seen ample evidence of her superior intelligence, and some measure of her strong will, too. We offer you—and all young parents—the blueprint for success, the only one that will work.

Children, obey your parents in the Lord, for this is right.

"Honor your father and mother"—which is the first commandment with a promise—

"That it may go well with you, and that you may enjoy long life on the earth."

Fathers, do not exasperate your children, instead, bring them up in the training and instruction of the Lord.

Ephesians 6:1–4
(italics mine)

Together with love, patience, and prayer, this is the perfect formula, but no one employs it perfectly. No daughter ever wanted to obey and please her parents more than you did, Cherry. And no parents ever wanted less to exasperate their kids than we did. You and Dan and Brittany may be more successful with this simple blueprint than we were, and nobody will be more glad than your Mom and Dad if you are. But chances are, your story will just be different, as ours is from all others. And chances are—no matter what—you'll go on loving Brittany the way we love you, unconditionally.

Mugwumps just seems to have that effect on ya . . .

DADDY

A Husband's Point of View
Dan O'Neill

It all began with such high hopes. Cherry and I built our relationship with the understanding that we could carve out a happy, healthy life together based on our many mutual interests and common faith. Sure, there were challenges to overcome but together we were certain that a conquest of life, including Cherry's anorexia, was meant to be. Looking back now, I marvel at the innocence and naive confidence with which we confronted one of medicine's most tenacious, death-dealing maladies. It was like climbing into a cage with a half-starved leopard.

After our first year of marriage a terrifying relapse of Cherry's seemingly tamed anoretic behavior struck almost without warning. Her long illness became a disillusioning experience in futility and depression for us both. Our pillar of hope cracked under the crushing weight of this mysterious disorder. Hope faded into a distant memory.

It is at this point that I must say, however, that if this book is built on any one theme, it is hope. In our darkest years it was the mere flickering memory of hope that, beyond our understanding, allowed hope itself to resurface as a point of light at the end of a dark tunnel. It was hope based on faith that provided the emotional energy for the long journey to health.

Although our movement towards healing appeared to be enveloped in a dense fog of pain and confusion, my own emotional response to the unfolding drama seemed to flow through six distinctive phases that bear a startling resemblance to Elisabeth Kübler-Ross's stages of dying. In her classic work *On Death and Dying,* Dr. Ross outlined the sequential stages of a terminally ill person's attitude towards dying: denial and isolation, anger, bargaining, depression, acceptance, and, finally, hope.

My own emotional reaction through Cherry's relapse and subsequent hospitalization was based, perhaps, on a kind of fear of death—the death of my wife or perhaps of our relationship. Such phobias are often difficult to define, which further contributes to the vaguely terrifying dimensions of the disease.

Denial, isolation. Our early months of married life, with a few notable exceptions, were filled with high expectations and lofty dreams. Cherry's protracted adolescent duel with anorexia nervosa seemed a thing of the past. Together we had put this hideous invader to flight. Our convictions of victory were deepened with each new testimonial of healing we gave at banquets, church services, even on television-interview programs. So it is no mystery that when Cherry's health began to deteriorate once again we should have tried to deny the obvious. We were afraid to even consider relapse as a possibility. After all, hadn't God Himself granted this recovery after much prayer by many people? We denied the facts and closed our eyes hoping that this thing would just go away.

At the same time, however, we also withdrew. This in itself was an admission that something was wrong. I began to turn down speaking engagements, lectures, and interviews. I became increasingly agitated by the inevitable observations, "Cherry certainly is thin. Is she losing more weight? She looks awful. . . ."

Find a cave, I thought, hide for a while, and let this storm blow over. Of course, there would be no such luck.

Anger. Ultimately, Cherry's relapse forced the obvious conclusion. Her health was worse than ever. The incredible feature of this stage was her repeated fervent denial of anoretic behavior. "I just have the flu," she would say. "I'm not trying to lose weight—honest!"

A kind of anger I had never known began to well up inside. I was angry with the situation in general—our lives were being plunged into turmoil. But resentment was also building towards my wife. How could she lie to me, her own husband? Particularly when it was so painfully obvious that she was not being truthful. Things began to take a bizarre turn in my own mind—I viewed Cherry as being unfaithful. She was having an affair, not with another man, but with food. Worse yet, she was denying it in the face of hard evidence! I was determined to catch her in the act and, to my disgust, I often did. She felt humiliation and fear. I felt betrayal.

Before long, anger spilled out in the form of volcanic wrath that frightened even me. Like an insanely jealous husband I confronted my wife, at first with questions and later with degrading, intimidating insults. "Are you an animal or a human being?" I demanded. "You've got a brain—use it!"

At that time I did not recognize her behavior as a manifestation of a deeper, underlying illness, but as carefully planned and concealed acts of aggression. In the early days of our relationship I was cool, objective, and almost analytical in my approach to Cherry's problems. I could afford to be compassionate—I had not yet become one of the victims. Once we were married the personal stakes were so much higher for both of us. Consequently, the situation became far more volatile.

I grew more animated with each new incident until finally I became physically abusive to the point of shouting, pushing, and throttling Cherry into confessing the truth. I discovered I was able to terrorize the facts from an otherwise uncooperative informant. Although these half-dozen or so heated scenarios never actually came to blows, a more subtle form of emotional damage was inflicted on us both: after each skirmish I was riddled with guilt and remorse while Cherry recoiled in fear and alienation. I could not see it at the time but I myself was becoming ill as I sought to tackle her disorder.

Bargaining. I knew that ultimately intimidation could not produce lasting change. As I attempted to refine my approach, we discussed regimens whereby I would supervise Cherry's eating, exercise, and weight. I adopted a reward system: "If you will just get your weight up to 105 pounds," I informed my 97-pound wife, "I'll take you to Jerusalem and Rome on my upcoming business trip."

The final result was the same as those of similar programs instituted by her parents years before: no weight gain. In fact, more precious pounds were lost. I had unwittingly recreated the same environment of control that had helped contribute to the problem in the first place. My bargaining technique actually proved counterproductive. I justified my authoritarian therapy by comparing it to cardiopulmonary resuscitation. Sometimes, to save a life, you must pound forcefully on the stricken person's chest. In my opinion we had a dying person in the house.

As I recollect now, I would have to admit to having bargained with God. It was the typical desperation prayer: "If you just get us out of this one, Lord, I'll do anything!" No such miracles were in store. The sickness would run its marathon course.

Depression. Cherry's hospitalization marked the end of hope for me. Our situation definitely had a terminal feeling about it. For the first time in my life I felt the deep despair of total depression. I had dreams of swimming in an unlighted tank full of black ink. I was drowning—helpless to alter what seemed to be certain tragedy.

Acceptance. Once one concludes that a situation is indeed helpless, the only recourse is to give up, to yield to the inevitable. I later learned from Dr. Vath that this could actually be a step forward for us. At least I was no longer complicating an already complex disease by maintaining an excessively authoritarian stance. Though I still loved Cherry, I had to release her to choose her own destiny— even if that choice meant death.

"Dr. Vath, how many times would you as a psychiatrist intervene to pull a suicidal person away from the ledge from which he threatens to plunge?" I asked.

"Two or three times, I suppose," he answered calmly. "Ultimately that person will have his way and there is very little we can really do in the face of his determination to die."

I knew I had to try to love Cherry through her illness, for that is how I had finally come to regard her condition—as a disease beyond her control. I would simply have to accept the outcome.

Hope. It was well into Cherry's therapy with Dr. Vath in the summer of 1977 when the first glimmers of hope beamed through the dark shroud. Ironically, it was in our most desolate hour that this mysterious optimism sprang forth. I am still not certain precisely what created it. Circumstances were certainly not improving—on the contrary, they were continuing to overpower us. Perhaps it was a grace from God. He knows we prayed enough. What is certain is that without hope our pursuit of life and liberation could not have endured.

For the incurably ill patient depicted by Dr. Ross, death is the end, the unavoidable final stage in the process of dying. Mercifully, our own process led to life, though this is not always the outcome for victims of anorexia nervosa. This bizarre malady entails a battle of life and death.

The early months of our crisis found us frantically searching for a magic remedy—some foolproof medical formula. The awful truth of the matter, we discovered, is that there is no quick fix or miraculous cure for anorexia. The key word is process—healing must be engaged as a process of first choosing, then moving towards *life*.

For us it became a journey, a pilgrimage that lasted for years. Our conversion to Catholicism was a profound lesson in the process of interior development, spanning the better part of a decade. We found that suffering, in spite of its pain, could be redemptive in that it builds character, tempered and forged in the fires of adversity. It produced new fibers of strength and resilience in our marriage and our individual personalities.

Cherry's conscious choice to live, the expert care of a loving doctor, the application of love, honesty, and compassion, all undergirded by our deepening faith in God, carried us from death to life.

A Medical Perspective
Dr. Raymond E. Vath

Anorexia nervosa is an illness characterized by behavior directed towards losing weight, peculiar patterns of handling food, intense fear of gaining weight, disturbance of body image, and, in women, amenorrhea. It is one of the few psychiatric illnesses that may have a course that is unremitting until death. There is evidence that anorexia nervosa has become an increasingly common and serious disease that merits much more attention from both the medical community and society at large.

When I began to encounter patients with anorexia nervosa early in my practice, I conducted an eclectic review of the psychiatric literature and attempted to integrate relevant issues into a holistic view of this highly complicated illness.

(1) The first issue I usually deal with in my patients is perfectionism. The anoretic maintains ideals and behavioral goals that are absolutely above reproach in order to avoid punishment or rejection. There is frequently a frantic striving to achieve, motivated by underlying guilt and remorse for failing to live up to expectations.

(2) Because perfection cannot be obtained, feelings of

inadequacy and unworthiness lead to an extremely poor self-image.

(3) The gender role is often rejected, sometimes because of a conflict between the patient and her mother or because the gender role is not validated by her father.

(4) As a result of the previous three issues, a pervasive depression emerges in which life becomes meaningless, hopeless, overwhelming. The anoretic feels sad and anxious and would like to give up. It is my opinion that the anorexia is a result of the depression and can be best perceived as a slow form of suicide, much as in alcoholism.

(5) The fifth issue that I deal with in therapy with the anoretic is an intense power struggle. Conflicts with others ensue as people try to prohibit the anoretic from engaging in self-destructive behavior. The tactic most often used is forced intimidation or guilt, the very approaches that lead to the quest for perfectionism in the first place.

(6) This is also related to the sixth issue, which is that of an interdependency that exists within the family in which the parents feel the need to be perfect. They attempt to control the patient into being a perfect child who makes them feel like perfect parents. They often look to the child for validation and gratification in some of their own areas of uncertainty. In this case it becomes difficult for the parents to allow the child to grow away from them. They are bound tightly to their child. On the other hand, the dominated anoretic has little confidence in herself and, therefore, views her family in a very ambivalent way, wanting to leave yet afraid to actually disengage.

(7) Deceptive practices are another factor to consider in treating the disorder. Secretive eating, vomiting, shoplifting, and denial are often behaviors adopted to elude the

power struggle and to attempt to escape criticisms when imperfections are uncovered.

(8) Finally, other physiological factors, such as endocrine abnormalities, either as a cause or as a result of the anorexia, must be evaluated. As the anoretic recovers, hormonal stimulation is sometimes necessary to aid in the return of normal bodily functions.

When Cherry first came to me as a patient, she had the typical emaciated appearance of the anoretic, was quite guarded, and surreptitiously uncooperative. My initial approach to clients with anorexia nervosa is to share with them the issues that must be dealt with as outlined above. As she began to measure herself against these, we found that in almost all areas, problems existed in varying degrees. (In this book Cherry has addressed every one of these issues in one way or another.) Our approach to the problem of anorexia nervosa has used family-therapy techniques coupled with cognitive approaches in which distortions are corrected. For example, the idea that people cannot tolerate disapproval was challenged, as was the belief that life above reproach is an attainable goal.

We challenged these unhealthy premises with four concepts that seem to be helpful. The first is that if an activity is worth doing, it is worth doing poorly because, second, practice will make better but not perfect. Third, it is better to try and fail than to fail by not trying. Fourth, we should fail at about half the things we do in life so we can discover our limits.

I remember vividly the day in therapy that I confronted the power struggle directly by asking Cherry's husband, Dan, if he felt he could really control Cherry's eating behavior. I still remember his thoughtful response when, after a minute's silence, he concluded that, indeed, he could not. Something seemed to transpire in that session because, in appointments that followed, there seemed to be a much more collaborative relationship between Dan and Cherry and improvement after that time seemed, in general, more rapid.

The bulk of these issues seemed to be resolved in about six months of intensive therapy, although I have worked as long as two years with other people with similar problems. Treatment became less intense over the next eighteen months—I saw them no more than three or four times a year. Improvement seemed to continue and finally, in 1979, I felt that Cherry had completely recovered. Her endocrine dysfunction was corrected, and now Dan and Cherry are the proud parents of their daughter, Brittany.

Because of the anoretic's perfectionism and intense secretiveness, I can measure Cherry's recovery not only by her appearance, but also from the observation that she is comfortable in going before the public, in writing this book, in granting newspaper interviews, and in appearing on television with her sincere desire to let other sufferers of this illness know more precisely what it is they are experiencing and, by the story of her own life, to give them hope that there is help for this malady. She has actively collaborated with me in therapy sessions with several of my patients, in a support group run by the Anorexia Nervosa Foundation of Washington, and she has assisted in teaching about anorexia nervosa at the University of Washington School of Medicine, and through media events. By using the family-therapy approach, not only has this illness not embittered her, but indeed it has made her a better person and improved her relationships with her husband, her parents, and the world around her.

APPENDIX

National Directory of Sources of Help

In addition to supplying valuable information, the following major national organizations, located in various regions of the country, will refer individuals suffering from anorexia— and those who love them—to local therapists and/or current support groups. I recommend them highly as resources for the kind of help so necessary for recovery.

—CHERRY BOONE O'NEILL

ANRED
(Anorexia Nervosa and Related Eating Disorders)
P.O. Box 5102
Eugene, Oregon 97404
Dr. Gene Ann Rubel

National Anoretic Aid Society
P.O. Box 29461
Columbus, Ohio 43229
Pat Tilton

NAANAD
(National Association of Anorexia Nervosa and Associated Disorders)

P.O. Box 271
Highland Park, Illinois 60035

American Anorexia Nervosa Association, Inc.
133 Cedar Lane
Teaneck, New Jersey 07666